WILD DUNEDIN

T0294440

NEVILLE PEAT & BRIAN PATRICK

WILD
DUNEDIN

THE NATURAL
HISTORY OF
NEW ZEALAND'S
WILDLIFE CAPITAL

OTAGO
UNIVERSITY
PRESS

CONTENTS

LEFT: Subalpine habitat on the flanks of Swampy Summit overlooking the city centre, Otago Harbour and the Pacific Ocean beyond. Prominent plants are three-finger *Pseudopanax colensoi*, inaka and mānuka. NP

BELOW RIGHT: Matriarch: the New Zealand sea lion called 'Mum' on Victory Beach. NP

First published 1995
Revised editions published in 2002, 2014 and 2019
Text copyright © Neville Peat and Brian Patrick

The moral rights of the authors have been asserted.

ISBN 978-1-98-853171-7

Publisher: Rachel Scott
Editor: Vanessa Manhire
Design/layout: Fiona Moffat
Maps: Allan Kynaston

Printed in China through Asia Pacific Offset

MIX
Paper from responsible sources
FSC® C136333
www.fsc.org

AWARD-WINNING 'WILD' SERIES

Wild Dunedin, the first book in a series of regional natural history titles covering the bulk of the southern half of the South Island, won the Natural Heritage Category of the inaugural Montana New Zealand Book Awards in 1996. *Wild Fiordland: Discovering the natural history of a world heritage area* and *Wild Central: Exploring the natural history of Central Otago* were national book award finalists in subsequent years. The fourth title, published in 2001, was *Wild Rivers: Discovering the natural history of the central South Island*. This 2014 edition of *Wild Dunedin* has been extensively revised and redesigned.

NAMES

The text is strewn with scientific names as well as common and, where known, Māori names. The widespread use of scientific names is intended to be educational.

Every described life form has a species name and a genus name, and sometimes a third name that identifies a subspecies or variety. Many people have three names (sometimes more), and their generic one is that which we call a surname. For fauna and flora, the genus name is expressed first.

However difficult some of the names may look, just remember that a little Greek or Latin goes a long way. If you have mastered such names as hippopotamus, rhododendron, rhinoceros, geranium, radiata and macrocarpa, why not extend your scientific vocabulary? Here is your chance.

PAGE 1: A kākā fledgling, Orokonui Ecosanctuary's first, 2009. Stephen Jaquiery / *Otago Daily Times*

TITLE PAGE: Spectacular Otago Peninsula – Lovers' Leap and The Chasm, with Allans Beach and Hoopers Inlet in the distance. NP

PREFACE

THE DUNEDIN REGION extends from the seashore to inland ranges. As the map shows, metropolitan Dunedin and its suburbs form but a relatively small part of the total area. This book is a comprehensive introduction to the landforms, plants and animal life of a city that professes to be the wildlife and nature heritage capital of New Zealand, a city with more than its fair share of rare and special elements.

Rather than list and illustrate every species of the flora and fauna native to Dunedin, we have selected the characteristic elements. Some of them will be well known to local people and to visitors; some are less obvious; some will be revelations. We have strived for balance. In this sort of work, invertebrate fauna is too often overlooked in favour of birds and the larger animals, and yet the invertebrate world is abundant, fascinating and full of zany forms and zany behaviour.

For the most part only indigenous species are described, and we give special emphasis to those species that are endemic to the Dunedin area. Clearly, introduced species have had an impact on the natural environment (for example, Old Man's Beard and possums) and we mention the most significant of them.

Following a chapter on the geology of Dunedin, which will intrigue Dunedin people who thought they had the measure of where they lived, the book describes things biological from the coast westwards. The chapter breakdown is geographically/ecologically defined, but nature does not recognise human boundaries, nor does it readily compartmentalise its offspring, so some species appear in more than one chapter.

The scientific expression 'type locality' appears in the book. Taxonomists use this expression in their descriptions of plant or animal species. It pinpoints the place where a particular species was collected from and first described, and where it might typically be found. The 'type specimen' or 'type population' will have come from such a place, providing a benchmark for comparing similar species.

Besides the descriptive content, the book discusses the conservation status of species that are rare, threatened or endangered, and offers some thoughts on what actions should be taken to conserve them and their habitats. The final chapter expands on this theme. For in the end, we must do more than simply record the elements of Dunedin that make it such a special place naturally. We want those elements to have a future.

NEVILLE PEAT AND BRIAN PATRICK

NORTH

LEGEND

	Dunedin City boundary	
	State highway	
	Other major roads	
	Taieri Gorge Railway	

A	Abbotsford		A	Burnside
B	Burnside		B	
C	Caversham		C	
FG	Frasers Gully			
WF	Whare Flat			
WG	Wingatui			

0   5 km   10 km

Otago Peninsula

Shag Point (Matakaea)

Palmerston

Waikouaiti
Waikouaiti Bay
Huriawa Peninsula
Karitane
Seacliff
Warrington
Rabbit Island

Derdan Hill
Mt Trotter
Mt Watkin Hikaroroa
Mt Royal
Swampy Hill

Macraes Flat

Nenthorn

Hummock

Swampy Hill
Mt Royal

Waikouaiti River Nth Br.
Waikouaiti River Sth Br.

Evansdale
Waitati
Mt Cargill

Orokonui Ecosanctuary

Port Chalmers
Otākou

Tairoa Head/Pukekura
Victory Beach
Okia Flat
Poatiru/Mt Charles
Cape Saunders

Harbour

Otago

Silver Peaks
Swampy Summit
Flagstaff
Central City
WF
FG
A B C

White Island (Pounuiahine)
Tunnel Beach
Black Head
Kaikorai Estuary
Green Island (Okaihae)

Painted Forest
Mt Allan
Pulpit Rock
Silver Stm
Mt Misery

Three O'Clock Stm

Taieri Gorge

Taieri River

Mt Hyde

WG

Saddle Hill

Ocean View
Brighton

Macraes Flat

The Crater
The Sisters
Billys Ridge
Taieri Ridge

Foulden Hill
Conical Hill

Sutton
Pukerangi

The Notches

Deep Stream

Hindon district

Clarks Junction

Lee Stream

Mosgiel
Outram
Allanton
Woodside Glen
Plain
Taieri
Manngātua Range
Mill Ck

Scroggs Hill

Henley
Otokia

Lower Taieri Gorge

Waihola
Lake Waihola

Taieri Mouth
Moturātā / Taieri Island

Hyde

Middlemarch
Sutton
Sutton Salt Lake
Sutton Stm
Strath Taieri Plain

Rock and Pillar Range

Summit Rock
Stonehenge
McPhees Rock
Old Dunstan Rd

Maniototo Plain
Taieri River

Loganburn Reservoir
Te Papanui Conservation Park
Deep Ck Park
Lammermoor Range

Black Rock
Nardoo Stm
Lake Mahinerangi

Dam
Waipori Falls
Waipori River
Waipori Gorge Scenic Reserve
Lake Waipori
wetlands

Waihola

Waitahuna River

CHAPTER 1

NATURAL HEART OF A CITY

THERE ARE FEW CITIES on earth that are as well endowed naturally as the City of Dunedin. One reason for this is its far-flung extent. It is a city that embraces large areas of farmland, lonely hills, upland plateaux, rugged river gorges and, yes, even an alpine zone – all this for a human population of just 125,000. It takes nearly two hours to drive from the city centre – the Octagon and its avenue of elegant plane trees – to the city's treeless, tussock-clad western boundary on the Old Dunstan Road.

Dunedin, all up, encompasses 3350 square kilometres – just over 10 per cent of the area of Otago. So it is big, but why so big? The answer lies in the reorganisation of local government in 1989, when metropolitan Dunedin spread out to embrace several boroughs and the Taieri and Silver Peaks County Council areas. The old counties contained the city's most important catchments for water supply, in particular the Deep Stream catchment, which has its origins in the Lammermoor Range. Thus water supply has had a major part to play in enlarging the city boundaries as far as the mountain ranges to the west. These ranges form the eastern margin of Central Otago, and today large areas are protected, notably

BELOW LEFT: Kōwhai flowers emblazon the cliffs above Leith Valley. NP

BELOW RIGHT: City limits. Sunrise strikes the rock outcrops on the summit crest of the Rock and Pillar Range, 1400m above sea level. NP

DUNEDIN BOTANIC GARDEN

The Dunedin Botanic Garden, which celebrated its 150th anniversary in 2013, features a range of native trees, shrubs, herbs and ferns in the Geographic Collection in the Upper Garden. Beside Lovelock Avenue is a rockery containing a diversity of subalpine and low alpine plant species. While most of the birds in the Botanic Garden aviary are exotic, it also breeds some endangered native bird species for release as part of a captive breeding programme.

in the Lammerlaw and Lammermoor Ranges, where the 21,000ha Te Papanui Conservation Park was created in 2003.

Of course, bigger does not necessarily mean better when it comes to natural history. But chances are that biodiversity will increase in proportion to area, especially if, as in Dunedin's case, the area takes in a variety of rock types, landforms, waterways, altitudes, climates and vegetation types.

Dunedin's overall climate is temperate, with rainfall generally adequate across the bulk of the city area and averaging 785mm a year in the city centre, with somewhat more in the hill suburbs. Mean temperature is 11 degrees Celsius. At the coast, temperatures are moderated by the sea; inland, summers are hotter and drier than at the coast and winters bring more frosts and snow.

Onshore winds from the northeast quarter are often persistent, banking clouds on the Mt Cargill–Swampy Summit skyline and churning up harbour waters. But the most feared winds are from the south or southwest. These are the gales that cultivate wind shear in exposed vegetation. A southerly front, approaching fast, can darken the sky in minutes and cause the air temperature to plummet by more than 10 degrees within an hour. The changeable nature of Dunedin's weather does have aesthetic compensations, though – the city is a spectacular place for cloud formations and variable lighting.

Weather is not the only changeable factor. Nothing in nature is fixed forever. There are shifts in vegetation patterns going on in many places around Dunedin. Examples are the slow, successional, uphill movement of shrubland on Flagstaff, and the wholesale takeover of the Green Island shrubland by taupata *Coprosma repens* following the dieback of *Hebe elliptica*, apparently through drought in the 1950s. Some changes are induced by burning off (after which native hard tussock may overtake more palatable native grasses) or mass application of fertiliser, which can cause widespread regeneration of matagouri in upland tussock grasslands.

The matagouri also responds to phosphate fertiliser by growing abnormally large.

Just as plant life adjusts to changing conditions, fauna can adapt, too. Some moths and butterflies have adopted introduced plant species as hosts for their larvae. Red admiral butterflies, for example, have taken a shine to introduced nettles. The New Zealand falcon has probably extended its range thanks to an increase in prey species provided by introduced passerine (perching) birds such as the starling and goldfinch. Fur seals and sea lions, virtually extinct on the mainland in the nineteenth century and for much of the twentieth century, are restaking claims on the rocky shores and beaches of Otago Peninsula.

Dunedin is best known for its royal albatross and yellow-eyed penguin, which have achieved iconic status nationally – even internationally. But surprises are in store for anyone who cares to look beyond these icons in the fauna. Take for example the royal spoonbill at Green Island and Taiaroa Head, or the South Island robin in the Silver Stream forest, South Island fernbird at the Waipori–Waihola wetlands, velvety peripatus crawling about Caversham Valley bush, clapping cicada in the Taieri Gorge, the Aoraia ghost moth navigating through forest at night, or the mountain weta confined to the harsh alpine zone of the Rock and Pillar Range, dependent on antifreeze in their blood to keep from seizing up.

The diverse and pulsating parade of wildlife knows no bounds. It is joined from time to time by new players, occasionally vagrant birds or insects far from their known range. Moreover, ongoing research is making discoveries of new species of insects at a startling rate. Since 1980, more than 30 Dunedin species have been named. Many more have been discovered but await formal description and naming. Likewise, new records for existing plants are liable to show up – and sometimes even new species come to light. In 2011 for example, a new skink, *Oligosoma burganae*, was described from a specimen found in the Burgan Stream area at the southern end of the Rock and Pillar Range. Dunedin can lay claim to

ABOVE: Aramoana, at the entrance of Otago Harbour, abounds in natural features – a large saltmarsh backed by salt meadow, parallel dune ridges and dune slacks, and impressive volcanic cliffs. The saltmarsh area enjoys protection as the Aramoana Ecological Area. In the distance are the hills of Otago Peninsula, including Mount Charles (408m), the highest point. NP

RIGHT: The Lower Taieri Plain from the subalpine shrubland/grassland zone of Maungātua. NP

BELOW: Meet Quammen, Orokonui Ecosanctuary's poster-boy takahē, pictured here drinking from a pond. Quammen and his mate, Paku, are ambassadors for their threatened species *Porphyrio mantelli*, which was rediscovered in 1948 in a remote Fiordland mountain valley. Takahē are enormous and highly colourful flightless rails, weighing up to about 4kg. They have an iridescent dark-blue head and breast and olive-green back, a massive scarlet beak, red legs and feet, and a brown eye. They can live to over 20 years. Quammen and Paku roam freely at the ecosanctuary but are often seen at a feeding station near the main entrance. NP

31 animals and plants that are endemic (see box on page 13). Nowhere else on earth do they occur. It is a list that will no doubt be added to as time goes by.

Dunedin city has long been a centre of biodiversity. A good place to start is the predator-fenced Orokonui Ecosanctuary, which opened in 2009 on Blueskin Road between Waitati and Port Chalmers (see page 82). On show in a semi-wild, free-to-roam setting is an outstanding array of birds and reptiles, including fauna not seen around Dunedin since the nineteenth century. Some rare and special 'lost' species – for example, takahē, Haast tokoeka kiwi, South Island robin, tuatara, Otago skink and jewelled gecko – have been reintroduced.

Because of the city's size and its range of habitats – from beaches of shining sand to frozen patterned ground in the alpine zone – Dunedin has more natural nooks left to be explored in depth than any New Zealand city. Moreover, it is much easier to find an alpine experience in Dunedin compared to North Island cities because the alpine zone is several hundred metres lower.

Although climate is an important influence on habitats and species, a more fundamental factor is the tectonic history, which gives rise to the rocks in the first place, and the age and lie of the land surfaces. So it is to geology we turn first.

LEFT: One of Dunedin's three endemic caddisflies, *Olinga fumosa*, which is a diurnal (daylight-active) species found in streams on the slopes of Swampy Summit. The smooth horn-shaped larval cases are attached to rocks in streams at mid-altitude. BP

OTAGO MUSEUM

Otago Museum's Nature galleries complex and its large landmark gallery Southern Land, Southern People provide an impressive introduction to the natural history – past and present – of Dunedin and the wider Otago–Southland region. *Southern Land, Southern People*, opened by the late Sir Edmund Hillary in 2002, explores the nature of the southern region through objects, words and images, from the geological and spectacular fossil history to the present day. A display of numerous moa species is world class, as is the exhibit of ancient marine creatures, including an 8m plesiosaur (New Zealand's largest fossil) and the fossil bones of ancient dolphins and penguins. The Nature galleries, refurbished more recently, present a diverse collection of animal life in colourful dioramas. These include the royal albatross, penguins and other birds, invertebrate life, fur seals and an enormous leopard seal.

DUNEDIN ENDEMICS

Plants (5)	**Locality**
Helichrysum intermedium var. *tumidum*	Otago Peninsula
Myosotis new species	Strath Taieri–Lammermoor Range
Celmisia haastii var. *tomentosa*	Rock and Pillar Range
Abrotanella patearoa	Rock and Pillar Range
Kelleria villosa var. *barbata*	Rock and Pillar Range

Moths (10)	
Gymnobathra new species	Lammermoor Range
Glyphipterix new species	Lammermoor Range
Gelophaula new species	Rock and Pillar Range
Kiwaia new species	Rock and Pillar Range
Tortricidae new genus and new species (3)	Rock and Pillar Range
Eudonia new species	Otago Peninsula
Ichneutica new species	Rock and Pillar Range
Meterana new species	Rock and Pillar Range

Caddisflies (3)	
Olinga fumosa	Swampy Summit area
Pseudoeconesus paludis	Swampy Summit area / Otago Peninsula
Oeconesus angustus	Lee Stream area

Craneflies (1)	
Zelandotipula new species	Dunedin forests

Harvestmen (2)	
Nuncia sublaevis	Dunedin forests
Prasma sorenseni regalia	Coastal Dunedin

Beetles (6)	
Prodontria montis	Rock and Pillar–Lammermoor Ranges
Oopterus new species	Lammermoor Range
Allocharis new species	Lammermoor Range
Irenimus similis	Lammermoor Range
Irenimus patricki	Lammermoor Range
Irenimus dugdalei	Lammermoor Range

Snails (1)	
Alsolemia cresswelli	Dunedin forests

Peripatus (2)	
New genus and species (2)	Dunedin forests (Caversham / Leith Valley)

Lizards (1)	
Oligosoma burganae	Rock and Pillar Range

2 | # THE UNDERLYING STORY A ROCK CONCERT

IF ROCKS COULD RESONATE, the land lying between the Rock and Pillar Range and the coast would produce a curious medley, for it is a land built of widely varying rock types, some ancient and slow to form, some born in a molten rush.

Can you hear the humming? Listen out for country-and-western tunes from schist outcrops inland, and sea shanties from coastal sandstone and other sedimentary rocks of marine origin. As for volcanic rocks like basalt, stand by for some heavy metal, hard and explosive.

The result of this diversity in rock types is an offbeat ensemble of landscapes and geological features.

The schist has the oldest ancestry, dating back some 200 million years. Its story begins on the seabed, with the gradual accumulation of sand and silt to form sandstone and siltstone kilometres deep. Over eons, compressed and heated, these rocks were transformed to schist, then slowly uplifted. Schist underlies everything – the layers of sedimentary rocks that came later and the relatively recent volcanic ones. The hills and ranges away from the coast are built of schist. It also extends seaward, a platform for the continental shelf adjacent to the coast.

Strange as it may seem, mountain ranges like Maungātua and Rock and Pillar are relatively new features on the landscape. Seventy million years ago the Dunedin region was very different. It was a peneplain of schist – fairly flat and lying close to sea level. The sea invaded this landscape. At times it was deep, at times shallow, and it left its mark in the form of sediments and fossils, layer upon distinctive layer, including limestone. Before and after this flooding by the sea, river gravels and swampy deposits added terrestrial imprints. In rocks just north of Dunedin, dating back more than 20 million years, there is fossil evidence of coconut palms.

About 13 million years ago, the coast convulsed with volcanic activity. Vents opened, there were ash showers, and red-hot lava flowed. The first eruptions were probably seated under the sea. This was no single cataclysmic event but rather a drawn-out process of sporadic eruptions and repeated flows – a 'shield volcano', built up over 3 million years. At Aramoana, no fewer than 25 flows have been identified in the cliff profiles. The volcano grew to be an imposing knuckle attached to the coast, perhaps reaching about 1000m at its peak – higher than the Maungātua Range (895m) and well above the present-day height of Mt Cargill (680m).

In the 10 million years since this volcanism transformed the coastal landscape and scattered volcanic features across the hinterland as far as the Maniototo, the forces of erosion have substantially reduced the hard core of the volcano. Port Chalmers, Portobello Peninsula and the mid-harbour islands mark its centre. A rift developed though the middle of the volcano that followed a line of weakness or

OPPOSITE: Ancient marine life was otherworldly and is nowhere to be seen today, except as fossils. Bottom to top: A long-snouted whale ancestor or *Archaeocete*; a turtle, similar to a leatherback, that roamed the Otago coast; and a large long-billed penguin that lived 30 million years ago. The rocks (bottom to top) are schist in the seabed (the oldest rocks), sandstone (marine sediments, about 20 million years old), basalt columns (about 11 million years) and schist again as alpine tors. Chris Gaskin

GEOLOGICAL TIMESCALE

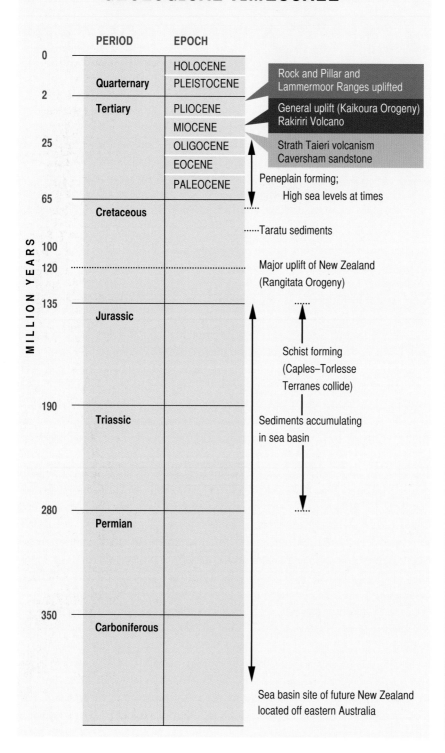

PERIOD	EPOCH
	HOLOCENE
Quarternary	PLEISTOCENE
Tertiary	PLIOCENE
	MIOCENE
	OLIGOCENE
	EOCENE
	PALEOCENE
Cretaceous	
Jurassic	
Triassic	
Permian	
Carboniferous	

MILLION YEARS

0
2
25
65
100
120
135
190
280
350

Rock and Pillar and
Lammermoor Ranges uplifted

General uplift (Kaikoura Orogeny)
Rakiriri Volcano

Strath Taieri volcanism
Caversham sandstone

Peneplain forming;
  High sea levels at times

Taratu sediments

Major uplift of New Zealand
(Rangitata Orogeny)

Schist forming
(Caples–Torlesse
Terranes collide)

Sediments accumulating
in sea basin

Sea basin site of future New Zealand
located off eastern Australia

EARTH'S TURN

A 10ha patch of hill country above North Taieri has a unique place in Otago's network of reserves: it is protected for its soil profile – a yellow-grey earth that has developed in loess (windblown silt).

Most yellow-grey earths have been modified by agriculture through drainage, cultivation, applications of fertiliser and pasture development or through forestry development. The Waiora patch, although grazed in the past, is largely unmodified and close to the altitudinal limit for this soil. Otago and Southland once had over 400,000ha of yellow-grey earths under forest or tussock vegetation.

The Waiora remnant is a benchmark for environmental impact studies. Under protection, the vegetation is expected to revert to mānuka, then to broadleaved trees and finally a podocarp forest featuring tōtara and mataī.

Yellow-grey earth development reflects the cold, dry climate of the last period of glaciation as well as the change to warmer, wetter conditions 10,000 years ago, when the land emerged from an ice age.

ROCK ART

As basalt in a lava flow cools, distinctive jointed columns are sometimes formed – as uniformly shaped and close-fitting as any Inca stonemason could have fashioned. This exposure of jointed column-forming basalt is at Black Head, on the coast just south of St Clair. Overseas and in Dunedin, outcrops of columnar basalt have become tourist attractions – Dunedin's Organ Pipes on the slopes of Mt Cargill are especially well known. There are also spectacular outcrops at Lovers' Leap and the Pyramids on Otago Peninsula, and at Black Head, where the rock columns meet the sea.

ABOVE: The overhanging volcanic cliffs at Black Head, south of St Clair, are a showcase for columnar basalt. They are protected under a covenant between the quarry company and the Department of Conservation. Safe public access to the outermost features is planned. NP

ABOVE: Natural symmetry – the columnar basalt formation near Mt Cargill known as the Organ Pipes. NP

LEFT: At Taiaroa Head, the tip of Otago Peninsula, there is a colourful display of volcanic rocks – a layer of dark grey basalt overlying a layer of reddish ash and volcanic rubble. The old Māori name for the headland is Pukekura, meaning red hill. Sean Heseltine

RIGHT: Caversham sandstone is strikingly exposed on the 30m-high cliffs near Tunnel Beach, between St Clair and Black Head. The sandstone is fossil rich, containing evidence of ancient marine life, including sharks and shellfish. Tunnel Beach is one of Dunedin's most popular walking tracks. NP faulting in the Earth's crust. When sea levels rose and the sea invaded this 'valley', Otago Peninsula became an island. Today it is reconnected to the mainland by a tombolo – the sandy flats of Tainui, St Kilda and South Dunedin. Otago Harbour and the city metropolitan area occupy the deeply eroded remnants of the volcano: witness the steepness of the arterial routes leading from the city centre – Caversham Valley Road, Upper Stuart Street and the Northern Motorway.

Volcanic rocks, chiefly dark grey basalt, overlie older sedimentary rocks such as Caversham Sandstone, Concord Greensand and Abbotsford Mudstone. There is an impressive example of this in Frasers Gully. In turn, the volcanic rocks are covered by a consolidated mantle of windblown silt and dust, called loess, which blew in from the central and western regions of Otago, and also from the riverbeds and estuaries east of Dunedin, at times when the continental shelf was exposed by lower sea levels. Around Dunedin the loess is often 1m deep. This lowering of sea levels occurred during the ice ages of the last 5 million years, when much of the world's water was locked up as ice caps and glaciers. Around Dunedin, the coast extended a long way east, and rivers cut gorges across the continental shelf.

Human timescale is but a blink in geological terms. The hills may look immobile today but nothing is fixed. Implying movement, fault lines crisscross the landscape, notably the Akatore and Green Island Faults south of Taieri Mouth and the Titiri and Maungātua Faults of the Taieri area. The hills and ranges beyond the volcano to the west are relatively young, pushed up only in the last 3 million years. And they are still growing. Still humming.

BELOW: Echo from the Eocene. Unlike any existing forms of penguin, this large long-billed specimen inhabited the Otago coast some 40 million years ago, when sea levels were higher. Its skull and bill, preserved in fine-grained mudstone, were recovered from Burnside cement works quarry. Of all the fossil penguins found in the southern hemisphere, the Burnside penguin is remarkable for the intact condition of its skull. It has yet to be formally described. Ewan Fordyce

FIERY ORIGINS

The same view, 12 million years apart. The aerial photo shows Otago Peninsula, Otago Harbour and the backdrop of volcanic peaks today – seen from the sea, with Rerewahine Point in the foreground and Taiaroa Head (Pukekura), the Mole, Aramoana and the harbour entrance at right. Papanui Inlet is partly visible at left. Saddle Hill is the peak in the middle distance. The skyline in the distance above Aramoana is formed by the Silver Peaks.

In the painting below, an eruption on the summit of Rakiriri, Dunedin's sprawling shield volcano, sends a cloud of ash seaward in its second eruptive phase, about 12 million years ago. Fresh lava flows have cut swathes through the forest and shrubland that grew up in quieter periods. Cones, domes and lava flows built up the volcano over 3 million years. Centred on the Port Chalmers area, it attained a height of about 1000m above sea level.

This portrayal is a view from the sea looking southwest. Because of erosion, only a few features are recognisable today, but it is helpful to compare the painting with the photo above. The circular vent in the foreground, one of numerous vents that formed on the flanks of the volcano, represents the Rerewahine Point area adjacent to Penguin Beach at the outer end of Otago Peninsula. The ridge stretching southwest represents the backbone of Otago Peninsula. Old, eroded phonolite lava domes, from which lava flowed to the sea, are slowly being covered in vegetation. The nearer ones now form the Kaika Hill area, just north of Victory Beach. Beyond are the domes of the Highcliff area. To the right of the ridge is a depression that eroded to become Otago Harbour. The active cones, one of which is spewing ash, mark the high ground of Mt Cargill and Mihiwaka. In the distance (left, centre) is volcanic Saddle Hill and below it an inlet. The hinterland is largely flat and well vegetated.

The first eruptions 13 million years ago built up a cone from below sea level. The second eruptive phase 12 million years ago spread ash and lava east, across what would become Otago Peninsula, and as far as Wingatui and Waitati. The final eruptive phase began about 11 million years ago, building the highest hills where the Mt Cargill group now stands.

RIGHT: Rakiriri, the ancient Dunedin volcano. The name derives from Rangiriri or Goat Island in Otago Harbour, which is more or less the centre of the volcano. Rakiriri, in the dialect of southern Māori, literally means 'angry sky'. The name is used here with the permission of Ōtākou Māori. There is no evidence volcanic activity will ever revisit Dunedin. The volcano is considered extinct. This is because the Dunedin area is no longer positioned over a 'hot spot', having been rafted away from the danger by the movement of the Pacific Plate, an enormous segment of the Earth's crust that is grinding slowly westward. Lloyd Homer/GNS (top photo); Chris Gaskin

A SUBTROPICAL TOUCH

Ten million years ago, in the vicinity of what is now Frasers Gully (off Kaikorai Valley), a freshwater lake formed on the southwest flanks of the Dunedin volcano. During quiet periods between eruptions, where the land had cooled, dense forest grew up around the lakeshore and spread across the lower slopes of the volcano. Galaxiid fish and small aquatic animals colonised the lake.

The climate was warmer then, nurturing a forest community reminiscent of the rainforests of modern New Caledonia or West Papua. She-oaks (*Casuarina*) and large-leaved southern beech (*Nothofagaceae*) dominated the canopy. Trees in the protea family and large-leaved coprosmas added a subtropical touch. Leaves falling into the still waters of the lake were preserved in the sediments formed from the silica remains of millions of microscopic algae called diatoms. The sedimentary material formed this way is called diatomite.

The fossil leaves and pollens contained in the Frasers Gully diatomite portray a forest strikingly different from the temperate one that exists today at midlatitudes (Dunedin lies in latitude 46 degrees south). In 10 million years, the forest flora of Dunedin has undergone wholesale change. Of 23 species discovered so far, only the beech has an existing close relative – silver beech *Lophozonia menziesii*. This ancient forest flourished at quiet intervals in the 3 million years of volcanic activity.

ABOVE: Fossil leaves (top), and fossil galaxiid fish from Frasers Gully, Kaikorai Valley. Ewan Fordyce

RIGHT: An artist's impression of the lake in Frasers Gully (off Kaikorai Valley), 10 million years ago.

Chris Gaskin/Department of Conservation

SCHIST | BONES OF THE EARTH

Beyond the volcanic core centred on metropolitan Dunedin and Otago Harbour is a landscape shot through with schist.

Near the coast the schist is shy, exposing itself sparingly, as on the tidal benches and low cliffs between Brighton and Taieri Mouth. Inland, however, schist makes a bold statement on the landscape, especially in the Strath Taieri and through the Taieri Gorge.

In districts such as Sutton and Nenthorn, the schist outcrops or tors evoke a strong sense of Central Otago. Where they line up as ridges protruding through the loess, the weathered outcrops resemble the ribs of some long-dead colossus, partly exhumed.

Schist is metamorphic rock, altered by heat and pressure deep in the Earth's crust. Otago's schist results from the collision of two large blocks or terranes of parent mudstone and sandstone 150 to 200 million years ago. The Torlesse terrane from the north collided with the southern Caples terrane.

Collision zone between the Torlesse and Caples terranes that formed Otago schist. From where it meets the sea at Brighton (SEE PHOTO ABOVE), the collision zone tracks inland to Alexandra, then on around the Wakatipu Basin to Mount Aspiring National Park. NP

ABOVE: A schist outcrop or tor on the Rock and Pillar Range. NP

The rocks in the middle were buried, squeezed and folded at depths of about 15km, and heated to temperatures of 400 degrees Celsius. The resultant schist was later lifted very slowly to the surface before being worn down by erosion to a nearly flat peneplain. Between 30 and 70 million years ago, when sea levels were high and a shallow sea covered East Otago as far inland as the Maniototo, much of New Zealand was also under water. New Zealand was an archipelago whose largest islands were probably in the south, formed from Otago schist and Fiordland granites. In more recent geological times, uplift in the landscape has excluded incursions by the sea.

Schist (derived from a Greek word meaning 'to split') is a layered rock that is prone to splitting and flaking. Wind, heat and ice all contribute to its slow decay. The quartz veins in schist, some of which are gold bearing, offer resistance to weathering.

The tors (upright schist outcrops) on the summit ridge of the Rock and Pillar Range overlooking the Strath Taieri are among the most impressive in Central Otago. Reaching 1450m at Summit Rock, the range is typical of the mountain formations of Central Otago, with a steep eastern face and a broad gently sloping western side.

Rock and Pillar, Taieri Ridge, Billy's Ridge and ranges to the west line up in parallel (northeast-trending) formation across Otago. They resemble pressure waves from the collision of two great plates of the Earth's crust. This collision, traced at the surface by the Alpine Fault on the western side of the Southern Alps, has crumpled and folded the surface of Central Otago, which lies to the east of the fault, on the Pacific Plate. The result is a ripple effect on a gigantic scale. Range and basin alternate, with the location and alignment of each successive range influenced by a deep-seated fault.

These ranges are considered to be less than 3 million years old – some 2 million years younger than the ranges that run close to but at right angles to them, notably the Kakanui Mountains and Hawkdun and Old Man Ranges.

The Otago schist collision zone reaches the sea at Brighton, where creamy or orange sand mingles with outcrops of schist in or just above the tidal zone. The schist here is 130–140 million years old.

EXPLOSIVE HISTORY

A lopsided depression or basin on Foulden Hill Station at the southern end of Taieri Ridge near Middlemarch is the only hint of a crater lake that once existed here. It is the product of a volcanic eruption some 20 million years ago, 7 million years before the great shield volcano began building on the coast.

BELOW: Farm shelter trees and green pasture mark the site of an ancient lake at Foulden Hill. NP

ABOVE LEFT: Leaf fossils from the Foulden Hill diatomite deposit near Middlemarch. NP
ABOVE RIGHT: Fossil turret shells. Ewan Fordyce

The crater formed after magma from a vent interacted explosively with ground water, which flashed to steam. As the explosions continued and more material was thrown out to form a lip or tuff ring, the hole grew steadily deeper. It is known as a Maar crater (after a region in Germany which has similar volcanic features). Rainwater filled it after cooling and the result was a lake about 1km wide and probably over 200m deep.

The lake became a forest-bound oasis for aquatic plant life. The stillness of the water was a feature, with drainage into it limited by the flatness of the surrounding peneplain. Tiny siliceous diatoms, green algae and freshwater sponges flourished and died – countless blooms and generations of them – and their remains sank gently to the lakebed, building up layers of sediment. As leaves from the fringing trees and shrubs fell into the water and sank to the bottom, they became encased in the sediment layers.

The leaves emerge today from the layers of diatomaceous earth as fossils, many of them breathtakingly intact and coloured in autumn hues. There are no trees of their species left. They are all extinct. Test drilling through the diatomite has reached 40m without finding the bottom of the deposit – an indication of the long life of the lake and the abundance of plant life in it. The deposits have been targeted for industrial use. Probably this lake existed for over 100,000 years.

Volcanic rock outcrops can be found on two features nearby – Conical Hill (Smooth Cone) and two knobs at the end of Taieri Ridge called The Sisters. Further north on Taieri Ridge is The Crater, which was formed explosively, like the one at Foulden Hill, and is much more recognisable as a crater. The sandstone remnants preserved in the vicinity of The Crater are a memento of an incursion by the sea, when the region was a peneplain. The sandstone has been dated at about 40 million years, but the volcanic rocks here are about 20 million years old.

ROCKY ODDS AND ENDS

- The complexity of Dunedin's geology has benefited commercial quarrying and mining companies down the generations. Among the resources exploited: sand, gravel, diatomite, lignite (brown coal), limestone, bluestone, basalt and gold.

- At Ocean Grove, Scroggs Hill and Allanton there are limestone deposits up to 10m thick, overlying coal seams. Limestone also outcrops at Sandymount on Otago Peninsula and Dowling Bay on Otago Harbour, where it is mixed with layers of ash that suggest that volcanic activity started while the limestone was being formed under the sea. Limestone comprises marine sediments, animal remains (fish, shells, etc.) and sometimes plant material in a cement of calcium carbonate.

- The much-admired creamy sand on Dunedin's beaches has come a long way. It is derived from the weathered schist of Central Otago. Over time, it has been transported down the Clutha River to the sea, then north along the coast by an ocean current – a process that continues today, although with much smaller volumes because of the entrapment of the sediment behind hydroelectric dams on the river at Clyde and Roxburgh.

- The Caversham tunnel on the main trunk railway line penetrates Caversham Sandstone that lies 250m thick under the volcanic rocks of Lookout Point.

- In August 1979, at the suburb of Abbotsford south of the city centre, a large block of sand and clay up to 30m thick and covering about 18ha, moved 50m downslope in half an hour – a natural disaster that was headlined around the world. Sixty-nine houses were lost in the Abbotsford landslide, and 450 residents displaced.

- Shale near Waitati is oil bearing. But no one has struck it rich.

- Coal seams, formed from plant remains in low-lying wetlands, occur in layers of sedimentary rock known as the Taratu Formation, which dates back 75 million years. Much of the commercially mined sand and gravel also lie in the Taratu sequence. The sand, mainly quartz, is valued for its decorative (white or cream) and hard-wearing nature. The quartz originated in the schist bedrock. Being schist's hardest component part, it was left after all the flaky parts were blown or washed away.

- Dark volcanic rocks with a greenish hue are phonolite. A good example is the massive outcrop supporting the Otago Peninsula Soldiers' Memorial off Highcliff Road, 225m above the harbour. Phonolite contains the mineral nepheline.

ABOVE: Erected on a massive outcrop of phonolite at Highcliff overlooking Otago Harbour is the World War I Soldiers' Memorial. NP

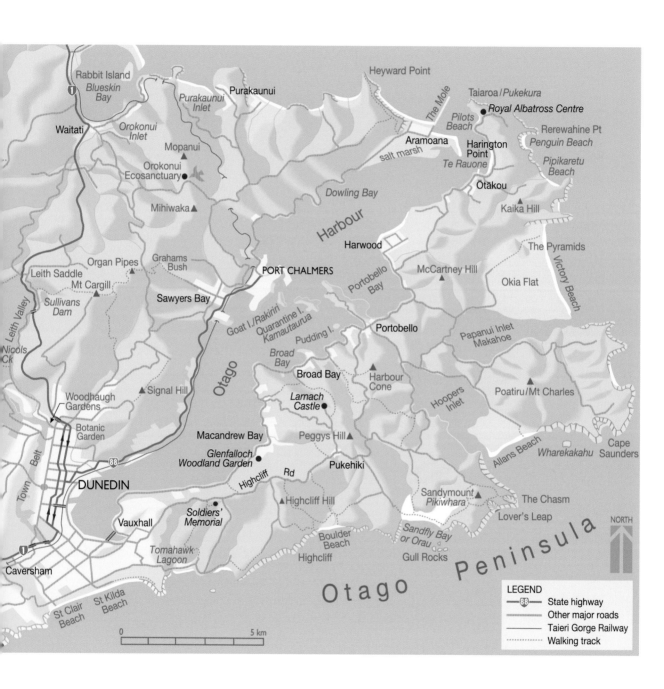

Rabbit Island
Blueskin Bay
Waitati
Orokonui Inlet
Purakaunui Inlet
Purakaunui
Heyward Point
The Mole
Pilots Beach
Taiaroa / Pukekura
Royal Albatross Centre
Rerewahine Pt
Penguin Beach
Aramoana
Harington Point
Te Rauone
Pipikaretu Beach
Mopanui
Orokonui Ecosanctuary
Mihiwaka
salt marsh
Ōtākou
Dowling Bay
Kaika Hill
Harbour
Harwood
The Pyramids
Organ Pipes
Grahams Bush
Leith Saddle
Mt Cargill
Sullivans Dam
Sawyers Bay
PORT CHALMERS
McCartney Hill
Portobello Bay
Okia Flat
Victory Beach
Leith Valley
Nicols Ck
Goat I./Rakiriri
Quarantine I. Kamautaurua
Pudding I.
Portobello
Papanui Inlet
Makahoe
Broad Bay
Woodhaugh Gardens
Signal Hill
Otago
Broad Bay
Harbour Cone
Poatiru/Mt Charles
Botanic Garden
Larnach Castle
Hoopers Inlet
88
Macandrew Bay
Peggys Hill
Allans Beach
Wharekakahu
Cape Saunders
DUNEDIN
Glenfalloch Woodland Garden
Pukehiki
Highcliff
Rd
Town Belt
Vauxhall
Soldiers' Memorial
Highcliff Hill
Sandymount
Pikiwhara
The Chasm
Lover's Leap
Caversham
Tomahawk Lagoon
Boulder Beach
Highcliff
Sandfly Bay or Orau
Gull Rocks
St Clair Beach
St Kilda Beach

Otago
Peninsula

NORTH

0   5 km

LEGEND
━88━ State highway
········ Other major roads
──── Taieri Gorge Railway
·········· Walking track

CHAPTER **3** | # OTAGO PENINSULA
NATURE'S FLAGSHIP

ABOVE: Wild coast – Allans Beach and Cape Saunders from the Sandymount Wildlife Refuge. Māhoe forest is in the foreground. The prominent hill is Mt Charles (408m), Otago Peninsula's highest point. NP

AN ISLAND in the distant past, Otago Peninsula retains an identity peculiarly its own. Given Dunedin's status as a wildlife capital, the peninsula is surely its central square, a showpiece area with flags flying boldly and colourfully – the flags of rarity, special character and spectacular appeal. From a sharp outer end called Pukekura (Taiaroa Head) right back to the imposing bluffs of Highcliff and Vauxhall, the peninsula is a gathering place for a strange mixture of animal life, some land-bound but much of it dependent on the sea. All roads lead to the peninsula, it would seem. 'Magnetic' is a word that springs to mind, but 'strategic' is rather more accurate.

The peninsula's indented shores lie close to deep water. Food is handy for the seabirds and marine mammals based on the beaches, rock platforms, cliffs and islets. Off the peninsula, a series of submarine canyons narrows the continental shelf and brings deep water as close as 10km to the land. North and south of the peninsula, the continental shelf widens to 30km. The canyons are thought to have been created at a time of lower sea levels in the last 5 million years, when rivers extended out over the continental shelf.

Today the sea is getting its own back. It makes deep inroads into the peninsula in the form of two large tidal inlets – Papanui and Hoopers. Their flatness within a landscape so hilly is surprising. The peninsula's highest hills, in the order of 300–400m, are noticeably lower than the Mt Cargill group on the opposite side of the harbour, which were formed later in the era of volcanism and have been eroded to a lesser degree. On the peninsula the hills are rounded and softened, a reminder that erosion, like rust, is persistent and, given time, will dismantle and transform a landscape. Helping to soften the landscape is a clay robe of loess – wind-blown silt.

The highest peaks are Mt Charles (408m), Peggy's Hill (395m), Transmitter Hill (381m), Sandymount (319m) and Harbour Cone (315m). Landslides on these and other peninsula hills continue the process of erosion. The peninsula is especially vulnerable to slips. Half of the area's 9000ha is at moderate to very severe risk of landslides. About 500 slip sites are recorded.

There are basically two sides to the landscape character of the peninsula: the ocean coast, wild and wave-tossed, where dark uncompromising cliffs of volcanic rock are interspersed with lonely stretches of fine shifting sand; and the harbour shoreline, mainly rocky and with many sheltered places, where the sea has a gentler impact and washes a rock wall protecting a main road and cycleways. A hilly backbone runs the length of the peninsula – about 20km. The peninsula reaches its maximum width of 10km on a line between Portobello Peninsula and Cape Saunders.

Human settlement has favoured the sun-catching harbour edge, much modified now by ribbon development connecting the settlements of Macandrew Bay, Broad Bay, Portobello, Harwood, Ōtākou and Harington Point. Harbour ferries served these places in the days before tarseal, when the peninsula was a backwater crowded with dairy farms. The dairy farms have gone but they left their mark in the form of pastures, some enclosed by drystone basalt walls, and shelter belts of Monterey cyprus (macrocarpa), the ubiquitous *Cupressus macrocarpa*. Highcliff Road, along the summit ridge of the peninsula, has some magnificent stands of these trees.

The ferry-borne visitors of yesteryear regarded the likes of Broad Bay as holiday resorts. Today's visitors are quicker moving and they come for different reasons. They come to see natural wonders – albatrosses at the world's only mainland colony, a private sort of penguin called yellow-eyed or hoiho, and the fur seals and sea lions that are making a comeback on the mainland. People are attracted, too, by landscape features such as the collapsed sea chasm of Lovers' Leap near Sandymount (a leap of 220m!) and the wave-worn stacks of columnar basalt behind Victory Beach known as The Pyramids. They also come to see built heritage in the form of Larnach Castle, 302m above sea level, surrounded by lawns, flowerbeds and tall exotic trees, and the woodland gardens of Glenfalloch, which retain elements of the native forest that cloaked the peninsula to the harbour edge. Glenfalloch's large mataī tree, several hundred years old, is an arresting reminder of the forest that once grew here.

Although farmland still dominates the picture, the surviving patches of native forest and shrubland are mostly under some form of protection. They are cherished not only for their component species, but also for their capacity to provide a home for penguins, jewelled geckos, red admiral butterflies and other fauna.

All in all, the peninsula is a nature precinct with a high profile. It is a busy natural crossroads – a flagship of biodiversity.

SEABIRD CITY

On the Otago Peninsula coast, seabirds and coastal birds abound. The air around Pukekura or Taiaroa Head is filled with shags (cormorants), gulls and albatrosses throughout daylight hours in the breeding season. As darkness falls, sooty shearwaters or tītī come home to their burrows, flying with swift, darting precision and an extraordinary energy for birds that have been out at sea fishing all day.

No two species fly alike. The shags are the commuters of this seabird city, going urgently about their business, often in line formation and flapping hard with necks outstretched. Gulls, floating on the wind, seem less driven by feeding or other schedules. Royal albatrosses, stiff-winged gliders of extraordinary size, perform graceful circuits of the headland, as if awaiting clearance from air-traffic control to land.

Three species of shag breed at this busy headland – spotted, Otago (formerly Stewart Island) and little. The smallest of them, little shags or kawau paka, feed in the harbour and nest in foreshore trees. Their roosting on boatsheds, ramps, powerlines and trees on the harbour edge of the peninsula is habitual. The regionally endemic Otago shag *Leucocarbo chalconotus*, found only on the southeast coast of the South Island, nests in tight colonies on pedestals of mud and vegetation. Their Taiaroa Head colony is the largest on the mainland with up to 400 nests, although numbers vary. Spotted shags or pārekareka nest on cliff ledges facing the ocean.

Sooty shearwaters or tītī (muttonbirds) go underground to breed, burrowing into sandy soils on suitable headlands. Because their mainland numbers have declined markedly through harvesting and land-use changes since the arrival of humans, the peninsula population is of vital importance.

Otago Peninsula is also a stronghold for yellow-eyed and little penguins. Yellow-eyeds, one of the world's rarest penguins, breed in shrubland on many of the peninsula's ocean beaches; unlike most penguin species, they stay based at their nesting areas after breeding is over for the year. Little penguins nest in burrows or rock crevices. Some 300 nests are found around Taiaroa Head, which

ABOVE: Pukekura Pā – an artist's reconstruction of Taiaroa Head 300 years ago, when a fortified village occupied it. Royal albatrosses are assumed to be breeding in the vicinity. The vessel returning home is a deep-sea fishing craft, a waka unua which specialised in catching barracouta.

Chris Gaskin/Department of Conservation

SEABIRDS AND COASTAL BIRDS BREEDING ON OR AROUND TAIAROA HEAD

1. Northern royal albatross / toroa *Diomedea sanfordi* NP
2. Royal spoonbill / kōtuku ngutupapa *Platalea regia*
   Sean Heseltine
3. Little penguin / kororā *Eudyptula minor* Sean Heseltine
4. Spotted shag / pārekareka *Stictocarbo punctatus*
   Sean Heseltine
5. Otago shag *Leucocarbo chalconotus* Sean Heseltine
6. Little shag / kawau paka *Phalacrocorax melanoleucos* NP
7. Sooty shearwater / tītī *Puffinus griseus* Sean Heseltine
8. White-fronted tern / tara *Sterna striata* Sean Heseltine
9. Southern black-backed gull / karoro *Larus dominicanus* NP
10. Red-billed gull / tarāpunga *Larus novaehollandiae* NP

holds the largest concentration in Otago and one of the largest in New Zealand. In addition, southern black-backed and red-billed gulls, the commonest seabirds on the coast, breed on many headlands on the peninsula. At Taiaroa Head, the red-billed gull colony is one of New Zealand's largest, expanding to 2200 nests in the 2012–13 summer.

Fewer in number, white-fronted terns nest on cliff edges and also, surprisingly, on wooden posts at the Mole opposite Taiaroa Head. Of slender build, they fly with superb skill, often dipping their bills into the sea in flight to take prey. Royal spoonbills have been breeding in trees on the ocean side of Taiaroa Head since 2002 – the first mainland nests on the South Island east coast. There have been up to 35 nests here.

All this seabird activity lends weight to New Zealand's claim to be the seabird capital of the world. No other country has a greater variety of seabirds breeding on its shores. More than half of the 160 native bird species breeding in the New Zealand region are seabirds, and Otago Peninsula is home to some of the most interesting.

ABOVE: A royal albatross incubating an egg at its Taiaroa Head nest. NP

THE ROYALS

Except for three species in the North Pacific and one based in the Galapagos Islands at the Equator, albatrosses are southern seabirds. Eighteen species, including the mollymawk group, breed in the south. No fewer than 13 of them breed in New Zealand's temperate and subantarctic zones, among them the largest albatrosses of all – the wandering and royal.

Buller's mollymawk *Diomedea bulleri* and white-capped (shy) mollymawk *Diomedea cauta* are occasionally sighted, patrolling inshore waters off Otago Peninsula. The term mollymawk is interchangeable with albatross.

The royal albatross or toroa is among the largest and most majestic of all seabirds, with a wingspan of about 3m and a flying style that enables it to traverse vast tracts of ocean quickly and efficiently.

There are two subspecies – northern and southern. Breeding is confined to the New Zealand region, although they range widely through the great Southern Ocean and probably circumnavigate it on a regular basis. More than 80 per cent of their lives is spent at sea, which is their tuckshop, watering hole and waterbed. The small Taiaroa Head colony was established by northern royal albatrosses, whose main breeding sites are found in the Chatham Islands, over 1000km northeast of Dunedin. Some 7000 pairs nest there. In 1938, when the first recorded chick flew from Taiaroa Head, there were three breeding pairs; now there are about 50. The total population (adults, sub-adults and juveniles) is about 200.

ABOVE: An adult royal albatross preparing to land at Taiaroa Head. NP

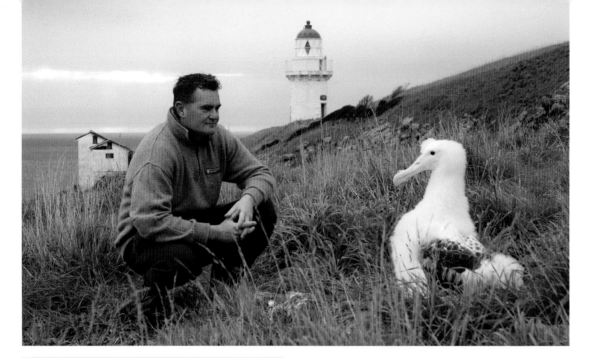

KEEPING TRACK

Since 1993, a few Taiaroa Head albatrosses have taken part in tracking studies that have shed more light on their migrations and foraging habits.

Tiny electronic packages, tuned to satellites, are attached to their backs and later recovered. Besides transmitting each bird's location, the packages measure air speed, barometric pressure, temperature and movements such as flying, feeding and sitting.

Studies suggest that early in the season the northern royals forage in continental shelf or shelf-edge waters off the Otago coast in waters 500m to 1000m deep, but later in the season they fly farther afield for food. In 2010, three juvenile northern royal albatrosses equipped with GPS were tracked all the way to Chile, a distance of 8500km. After fledging from Taiaroa Head they flew northeast, parallel to the coastline, then headed east across the South Pacific. Their daily distances reached 1047km, at speeds of up to 110km per hour. The first bird arrived in Chilean waters, a customary feeding ground for northern royal albatrosses, in 16 days; the longest took 34 days. They stayed between latitudes 23 and 58 degrees south and remained within 100km of the land.

Information from this and similar experiments elsewhere in the Southern Ocean assist scientists who study the alarming bycatch of albatrosses killed by deep-water longline fishing operations (when the birds scavenge for bait and are hooked). Conservationists have campaigned for years to change fishing gear and practices in an effort to reduce the albatross bycatch.

Royal albatrosses are long-lived and slow to reproduce. They may not start breeding until they are 8–10 years old and, if successful, will raise only one chick every second year. They 'holiday' at sea between breeding years. The breeding season starts in October, with their arrival back at the colony and a reuniting of the pair. Eggs are laid in November and incubated for about 80 days – a world record for seabirds. The chick is guarded and fed by each parent in turn for the first five weeks, after which both parents are fully employed catching food for it. At fledging, usually in September, the chick may be heavier than its parents, at over 8kg. When it eventually takes to the air, it will spend at least three years at sea before returning to the colony.

Squid are prominent in the diet of royal albatrosses, which feed by seizing prey at the surface, often at night. Up to a quarter of the diet of Taiaroa Head-based birds is octopus, much of which is probably scavenged from fishing boats. The royal's large bill is adapted for hooking and slicing squid. The tubes at the top are nostrils, through which excess salt is drained from the bird's salt glands.

The Taiaroa Head albatrosses have been continuously studied for decades – longer than any other seabird. A female banded as an adult breeding bird in the 1930s lived for over 60 years, setting a world age record for a wild bird. 'Grandma' disappeared in 1989, with a chick left at the nest. The chick fledged, thanks to some hand feeding, and has since returned to the colony as a juvenile.

Few of the world's seabirds are as intensively managed as Dunedin's royals. Although free to come and go, they are closely monitored. Eggs are weighed to check for infertility; hatching is assisted occasionally; chicks are weighed and orphans assigned foster parents; supplementary feeding is instituted when required. In addition, routine trapping is carried out for predators (cats, ferrets, stoats, rats) and precautions are taken against flystrike at hatching time.

As a result of this hands-on management by Department of Conservation staff at the 5ha Taiaroa Head Nature Reserve, the royal albatross population has benefited considerably. About 40 per cent of the nests have been actively managed over the years.

Breeding was established in 1938 following the protective work of a Dunedin teacher and seabird researcher, Lance Richdale, who became a world authority on albatrosses and penguins. Since 1972, the nesting area of the royals has been open for public viewing.

SUBURBIA FOR SHAGS

Surrounding the royal albatross colony on every side are the nesting areas of three shag (cormorant) species, each requiring a different habitat.

On the cliffs on the ocean side, sleek spotted shags plait nests of seaweed, usually on narrow ledges and about 1m apart. On average, three eggs are laid, but breeding success varies. Every few years adults die in significant numbers, probably because of a sudden decline in their food resources. They prey on schools of small fish over the continental shelf, diving foot-propelled to about 20m, usually in groups.

The recently renamed Otago shag, largest of the three species (wingspan 1.2m and up to 3kg in weight), nests on columns of mud-compacted seaweed and grass up to half a metre tall. One or two chicks are fledged per nest. There are pied and bronze (entirely dark) forms, and about 2000 of them in all. In 2016, through genetic studies, scientists separated the Otago shag from its Foveaux Strait/Stewart Island cousin *Leucocarbo stewarti*.

Like spotted shags, Otago shags feed mainly at sea. They can stay submerged for up to three minutes while diving to at least 50m in pursuit of bottom-dwelling fish as well as mid-water ones.

OPPOSITE (TOP): Lyndon Perriman, head (2001–17) at the royal albatross colony at Taiaroa Head, checks out a five-month-old chick. It has four months to go till it fledges and departs the colony for its juvenile years at sea. NP

OPPOSITE (BELOW): A five-month-old royal albatross chick is weighed by rangers Lyndon Perriman (left) and Colin Facer at Taiaroa Head. NP

SET NET THREAT

Monofilament gillnets, set to catch fish in Otago Harbour or off the coast, can entangle and drown marine fauna such as shags, penguins, dolphins and seals.

Spotted shags, which enter Otago Harbour seasonally in large groups in pursuit of shoaling fish, are especially at risk. Yellow-eyed and little penguins have also been killed in nets in the past, while commuting between their beaches and offshore feeding grounds.

As a result of the toll on non-target species, set nets are banned from designated sections of the peninsula coastline and parts of Otago Harbour, notably around the harbour entrance.

Little shags, weighing under 1kg, nest in trees on the headland, being essentially harbour-dwelling. They lay three to four eggs. For unknown reasons, only about half the adult population on the harbour will breed in any one year.

Typically seen roosting on trees or structures overhanging the water, little shags dive for fish to depths of about 5m. Their dives last up to half a minute. They are often seen with wings hung out to dry. Their plumage is black and white – black backs, white fronts – although the degree of white on their undersurfaces varies.

ABOVE: Otago shag colony, Taiaroa Head. NP

LEFT: Spotted shags nest precariously on cliff ledges at Taiaroa Head. NP

LITTLE PENGUIN | SMALL IS BEAUTIFUL

Little (formerly blue) penguins or kororā nest at several places on Otago Peninsula, but nowhere as abundantly as at Taiaroa Head. In the mid-1980s there were only 30 to 50 nests; within 10 years the number had jumped to 200; and by 2013 there were at least 300, thanks to increased predator control associated with improved visitor facilities at Pilots Beach and after-dark guided tours.

The smallest penguins of all, little penguins *Eudyptula minor* weigh just over 1kg and have a body length of about 30cm. They are found throughout New Zealand, although predation by cats, dogs and mustelids (ferrets, stoats, weasels) has reduced their numbers significantly on the mainland. Predator trapping at Taiaroa Head to protect the royal albatrosses has probably benefited the population. Wooden nesting boxes have been installed to encourage them and provide further protection.

Little penguins nest in burrows or caves, often in association with other burrowing seabirds, and they set out to raise a brood of two chicks – and sometimes a second brood in the same year. At sea, usually in groups, they pursue mid-water fish and squid. Still in groups, they return to shore after dusk. Their loud screeching and braying calls at night have made them unpopular with some crib owners.

BELOW: The little penguin is vulnerable to terrestrial predators but responds well to protection.

Craig McKenzie

ABOVE: Two yellow-eyed penguin chicks, half hidden in flax, await the return of their parents with food. NP

CENTRE: A moulting adult yellow-eyed penguin (left) with a fledgling. Moulting occurs after the chicks have fledged. NP

HOIHO | A PRIVATE SORT OF PENGUIN

Otago Peninsula is a stronghold for the endemic yellow-eyed penguin or hoiho. Colonies on the peninsula's ocean side represent 40 to 50 per cent of the mainland population, although mortality events over the years can hit hard.

At 370cm tall and over 5kg in weight, hoiho is the largest penguin living in a temperate region – the South Island's east coast and Stewart Island. Yellow-eyeds also breed at the subantarctic Auckland Islands and Campbell Island. Periodic declines in population – due to food shortages, biotoxins in the food web or predation by mustelids, dogs and cats at mainland breeding areas – have prompted the species to be dubbed the world's rarest penguin.

Unlike most of the world's 18 penguin species, hoiho prefer to nest out of view of neighbours. They nest on the ground in coastal dune vegetation, shrubland or forest and will walk hundreds of metres, over sometimes steep terrain, to reach a suitable nest site.

A non-migratory species, they tend to go to sea during daylight hours to feed and return to the breeding area, their natal site, in the late afternoon. During the breeding season their routines may vary. Yellow-eyeds usually mate with the previous season's partner. Two eggs are laid by September, with the six-week incubation shared. Chicks are guarded by the parents in turn for about six weeks, then left by themselves during the day while the parents go out fishing. Fledging occurs some 15 weeks after hatching. Juveniles typically test out their brand-new feather wetsuits with a journey north, as far as the Cook Strait region, in their first year.

After February, when the chicks fledge, the adult birds fatten themselves in preparation for their annual moult. They must stay out of the water for about two weeks, until their old feathers have been replaced entirely by a new set. During moulting the birds may appear unwell. They are vulnerable to dog attacks and fire at this time. If chased into the sea without their insulating feathers intact, they will die of exposure.

Hoiho, the yellow-eyed, is the best known of the six penguin species breeding in New Zealand – three on the mainland (yellow-eyed, Fiordland crested and little), three in the subantarctic zone (Snares crested, erect crested and rockhopper).

It is also the most distinct penguin scientifically, justifying a genus of its own – *Megadyptes antipodes*, meaning large southern diver. It is the least adapted in size, bone structure and feathering of all the penguins; in other words, it is the penguin most closely related to ancestral members of the family. New DNA studies on penguin bones from early Māori ovens and middens indicate a larger previously undescribed species, now known as *Megadyptes waitaha*, inhabited mainland New Zealand before the yellow-eyed. After it died out, yellow-eyeds became more abundant in the Waitaha penguin's range around southern New Zealand.

Penguins go back a long way. Fossil discoveries in New Zealand point to a 'proto-penguin' that lived 50 to 60 million years ago. It almost certainly evolved from seabirds that flew. Since then, penguins have adapted in astonishing ways to become the bird world's most accomplished swimmers and divers.

Since its rarity and unusual nature came to public notice in the 1980s, the yellow-eyed penguin has become a nationwide symbol of conservation. The Yellow-eyed Penguin Trust was launched in Dunedin in 1987 in response to concern about the future of the species on the mainland. That concern was highlighted by population studies of mainland colonies undertaken by Otago Museum zoologist John Darby, starting in 1980 and following on from the pioneering work of Lance Richdale. In the years since its formation, the trust has been a rallying point for wide-ranging conservation efforts.

Conservation strategies include habitat purchase, revegetation programmes, nesting boxes, predator trapping, ongoing scientific studies, fundraising and education.

ABOVE: An adult yellow-eyed penguin negotiating coastal vegetation on Otago Peninsula while returning to its nest after a day at sea. NP

VARIABLE OYSTERCATCHER | 'BEACHMASTER'

The bird world's equivalent of a beachmaster is the variable oystercatcher or tōrea-pango *Haematopus unicolor*. Commonly called black oystercatcher, it sets up territories along Otago Peninsula beaches in the breeding season (November to January), and expresses annoyance at any intrusion – a sharp piping call. Two or three eggs are laid in a simple nest, often nothing more than a scrape in the sand at or just above high water.

Most sandy beaches on the peninsula are packed with black oystercatcher territories, shoulder to shoulder. The variable oystercatcher comes in a pied form, but black ones prevail in southern New Zealand. The pied variable may be confused with South Island pied oystercatcher but the latter is in fact a different species, almost always nesting inland.

In winter, black oystercatchers gather in flocks to feed. Regular low-tide haunts include the rocky intertidal zone at Vauxhall and the beach at Te Rauone. At high tide they invade sports fields, including the one at Tomahawk, in search of worms, grubs and other invertebrates.

RIGHT: Close-up of the head of a variable oystercatcher.

Sean Heseltine

BELOW: A variable oystercatcher relaxes at Pilots Beach in the company of red-billed gulls and paradise shelducks. NP

MARINE MAMMALS | CRUISING

Marine mammals – fur seals, sea lions, dolphins and whales – are attracted to the waters around Otago Peninsula for the same reason that seabirds congregate here: food supply.

New Zealand fur seals are now plentiful in the area. In small numbers, New Zealand (Hooker's) sea lions (whakahao) are beginning to make their presence felt on the beaches. Other occasional visitors to peninsula and city beaches include leopard seals (popoiangore) and elephant seals (ihu koropuku). Dolphins and whales are less obvious – unless they strand.

Three species of dolphin enter Otago Harbour occasionally – dusky, bottlenose and common. Dusky dolphins, the most commonly encountered species in New Zealand coastal waters, are relatively abundant off Otago in winter and spring. The dolphins that swim up the harbour as far as Dunedin are most likely to be bottlenose dolphins, or the smaller common dolphins, which may perform spectacular leaps.

Orcas (killer whales or maki) are rarer off the peninsula. Pods of as many as 12 orcas occasionally cruise around the Otago Harbour entrance. Southern right whales have been seen inside the entrance in the past. Before commercial whaling slashed their numbers, they are thought to have used the sheltered waters of the harbour for calving.

ABOVE: A southern right whale wallowing off Tomahawk, Otago Peninsula in winter. Right whales swim slowly – four knots is a sprint. They feed on krill. Graeme Loh

ABOVE: New Zealand fur seals. NP

BELOW: A young New Zealand fur seal snoozing on rocks at Pilots Beach. Fur seals have a pointed snout, long whiskers and small external ears. Colonial breeders, they also congregate outside the breeding season. NP

NEW ZEALAND FUR SEAL | A FLOURISHING ACT

Otago Peninsula is a showpiece area for the New Zealand fur seal *Arctocephalus fosteri* (kekeno).

Before 1970 the fur seal population was small and scattered. Breeding began about 1980 and has been steadily increasing since. There are now breeding colonies all along the peninsula, notably at Cape Saunders and Taiaroa Head, as well as numerous haul-out sites. In the mid-1990s the various colonies produced about 1200 pups altogether and the peninsula continues to host one of New Zealand's largest fur seal populations.

For breeding habitat, fur seals favour sea caves and rocky shelves out of reach of waves. Haul-out sites, including gravel beaches and rock islets, may be more exposed. Adjacent grassy or tussock-clad slopes are often used for resting, sleeping or convalescing from injuries.

From late October breeding males, weighing up to 185kg, set up territories and fight hard to hold them. Females give birth in December, mating with the territory-holder about a week later. The pup is dependent on its mother for almost a year. Tagging studies suggest there is some movement between Otago Peninsula and the West Coast. Males disperse northward after breeding but females, which are difficult to tell apart from sub-adult males, stay within range of the breeding sites. Numbers peak in late summer.

Fur seal populations are in the process of recovering from mainland extinction by Māori hunters in pre-European times and by early European sealers. Eventually, their numbers will be limited by the availability of suitable breeding habitats.

Arrow squid and octopus make up more than half the diet of fur seals, which feed mainly at night. Diving to over 200m, they also eat fish, mainly hoki, barracouta and lanternfish.

ELEPHANT SEALS

Southern elephant seals *Mirounga leonina* visit Otago Peninsula occasionally. Taiaroa Head and Te Rauone Beach at Harington Point are among the haul-out sites for these seals, which can become traffic hazards on Harington Point Road.

Elephant seals haul out on sand or gravel beaches to breed, moult or rest. While moulting (skin and hair peels off in patches), they may stay out of the water for a couple of weeks. The nearest breeding site is Nugget Point, South Otago, but most breeding occurs on subantarctic islands.

They are the world's largest seal, with adult males reaching over 5m in length and four tonnes in weight. They have an enlarged nose or proboscis, from which they get their name. Females are much smaller. On land, elephant seals are slow and cumbersome, resembling giant caterpillars, but at sea they can dive to depths of over 1km in pursuit of fish and other prey.

NEW ZEALAND SEA LION | COMEBACK STORY

The rarest of the world's five sea lion species, New Zealand (Hooker's) sea lion or whakahao *Phocarctos hookeri* is making a comeback on mainland New Zealand – and Otago Peninsula is centre stage.

Eliminated by Māori hunters from the mainland before the arrival of Europeans, these sea lions are seen singly or in small groups on the Peninsula's sandy beaches and dunelands.

They may appear on any beach, with 20 to 30 ashore at any one time on Otago Peninsula and a similar number hauling out on South Otago (Catlins) beaches. Unlike fur seals, they are not intimidated by people and usually remain indifferent. But if approached too closely or harassed, they may charge. On flat, hard sand they run as fast as people. Their presence has prompted the Department of Conservation and the New Zealand Sea Lion Trust to warn visitors to these beaches to stay at least 10m from hauled-out sea lions and keep dogs under control. Small numbers of pups are produced each year.

PERFORMING IN THE WILD

One of the best places to view fur seals from land is at Taiaroa Head.

On the headland's ocean side, the seals haul out onto broad rock platforms and are commonly seen frolicking in tidal rock pools or swimming along the shore. Close-up viewing is available at Pilots Beach on the harbour side of the headland, a favourite haul-out site for males young and old.

Harbour cruise vessels offer good views of the seals from the water.

ABOVE: Elephant seal. NP

ABOVE: New Zealand sea lions on Papanui Beach. NP

RIGHT: The sea lion matriarch known as Mum had most of her pups at Taieri Mouth and swam them north to Otago Peninsula when they were old enough. Here she is with her eighth pup at Taieri Mouth. NP

ABOVE: A male sea lion at Allans Beach roars his objection to being disturbed. NP

The majority of sea lions on peninsula (and south Otago) beaches are young males – migrants from the species' main breeding sites in the subantarctic Auckland Islands. Bulls can weigh over 400kg – twice the weight of fur seal males – and reach about 3m in length, with long hair over neck and shoulders forming a lion-like mane. They are distinguished from fur seals by their greater size, blunt head and short whiskers. Their gait differs, too. Fur seals gallop; sea lions march steadily on all fours, moving their legs in turn. Female sea lions, much smaller and paler than adult males and sometimes creamy, are difficult to tell apart from males under two years of age.

Sea lions prefer sand to rock. A layer of blubber (rather than fur) insulates them, and to keep cool when ashore they often hunker down in the sand and flick it over their backs with their flippers, till they are almost buried.

Diet studies identify squid, barracouta, red cod, flounder and jack mackerel as important fish. Skate, octopus and paddle crab also feature in sea lion diet. Like fur seals, sea lions are highly agile in the water and dive to over 200m.

The total population of New Zealand sea lions is in the range of 8000–12,000. Alarm over the numbers being caught in the nets of squid trawlers operating in subantarctic seas has led to changes in fishing gear and practices.

PENINSULA PLANT LIFE | EXCLUSIVE ELEMENTS

In keeping with the distinctive nature of the fauna and the island atmosphere of the place, plant life on Otago Peninsula boasts some exceptional and exclusive elements.

As one might expect of a large island, the vegetation map is a mosaic of plant communities, ranging from cliff vegetation and coastal turf through shrublands on dunes, damp places and drier slopes to forests of flowering trees and, the oldest community of all, tall podocarps. The suite of trees and shrubs (including the shrubs *Corokia cotoneaster*, *Helichrysum lanceolatum* and *Carmichaelia petriei*) is commensurate with a drier and sunnier climate than that found on the higher, wetter hills on the other side of the harbour.

The good news is that diversity still rules; on the sadder side is the fact that little more than a tenth (about 1000ha) of the peninsula is still forested, only half of it native.

Tall forest once clothed the peninsula to the cliff edges and dunelands, dominated by the magnificent podocarps – rimu, miro, mataī, tōtara and kahikatea. Most of it was felled for building timber and fence posts following European settlement, and pasture was sown in its place.

Once the predominant community, podocarp forest is now the rarest. On the lower slopes of Harbour Cone (Hereweka) overlooking Hoopers Inlet is the last surviving stand of rimu *Dacrydium cupressinum* – a grove of about 60 trees up to 15m tall and half a metre in trunk diameter. Interspersed with some 10 large

ABOVE: This stand of podocarp forest, featuring rimu and pōkākā, on the lower slopes of Harbour Cone / Hereweka overlooking Hoopers Inlet, is unique on Otago Peninsula. Protected by private covenant, the forest remnant provides habitat for the diminutive rifleman, which survives at a few places on the peninsula. In this patch nesting boxes are put out for the riflemen. NP specimens of pōkākā *Elaeocarpus hookerianus*, the rimu survive amid a 10ha patch of kānuka-dominant bush, the whole a fetching snapshot of the Otago Peninsula of old, with animal life to reinforce the picture. The rimu enclave is home to families of rifleman, a native bush bird, New Zealand's smallest. Less obvious is a species of lacewing peculiar to podocarp forest.

The peninsula's largest patch of native forest is Taiaroa Bush, covering 42ha of hillside bordering Okia Flat. The large podocarps have gone (there remain only a few small examples of Hall's tātara *Podocarpus cunninghamii* and matāi or black pine *Prumnopitys taxifolia*), but the peninsula's commonest native trees are here – the ubiquitous māhoe or whiteywood *Melicytus ramiflorus*, coastal-dwelling ngaio *Myoporum laetum*, gully-hugging tree fuchsia or kōtukutuku *Fuchsia excorticata*, and broadleaf *Griselinia littoralis*. Broadleaf tolerates most conditions, including dry sites on its own. Narrow-leaved lacebark *Hoheria angustifolia* is among the tallest trees of Taiaroa Bush. Kōwhai *Sophora microphylla* gilds the forest in spring with its flowers.

Other flowering trees here, all of which produce berries, are milk tree or tūrepo *Streblus heterophyllus*, putaputaweta or marbleleaf *Carpodetus serratus*, and wineberry or makomako *Aristotelia serrata*. Among the shrubs, the coprosmas are well represented by *Coprosma areolata*, *C. rubra* and *C. crassifolia*. The vines of supplejack *Ripogonum scandens* and *Muehlenbeckia australis* add a tangled, unruly appearance.

Overall, though, the understorey has been too exposed to stock from adjacent farmland over many years to develop its natural complexity – a familiar experience for patches of native bush in many other parts of the peninsula.

Across the peninsula, gullies too steep to plough, or too shady and damp to be of much use to farming, are refuges for shrubs and small trees. Among the common species are the coprosmas *Coprosma propinqua* and *C. rotundifolia*, kōhūhū *Pittosporum tenuifolium*, mingimingi *Leptocophylla juniperina*, pepper tree or horopito *Pseudowintera colorata*, māpou *Myrsine australis* and koromiko or New Zealand veronica *Hebe salicifolia*.

At Sandymount, south of Hoopers Inlet, there is a real mixture of plant communities – low forest dominated in turn by ngaio and māhoe, a 10ha stand of kānuka, and clifftop and coastal shrublands featuring *Coprosma crassifolia*, *Hebe elliptica*, fierce lancewood *Pseudopanax ferox*, *Corokia cotoneaster* and the tree nettle or ongaonga *Urtica ferox*. Tree daisies are plentiful here – *Olearia arborescens* and *Olearia avicenniifolia*. Both present bold showings of honey-scented white flowers, clouds of them – *O. arborescens* in early summer, its cousin at the end of summer.

On the southern side of Portobello Peninsula is a tree daisy anomaly. Clinging to cliffs near the Portobello Marine Laboratory are specimens of *Brachyglottis rotundifolia* or muttonbird scrub, which is possibly out of place here and may have been introduced some decades ago. A relative of muttonbird scrub, but with vastly different form, is the yellow-flowering liane *Brachyglottis sciadophila*. It is one of Otago Peninsula's special plants – a rare species close to its southern limit. Native scrambling species do well on the peninsula, with gaps having opened up for them as a result of the decimation of forest and the regrouping of remnant patches. The list includes climbing rātā *Metrosideros diffusa*, native jasmine *Parsonsia heterophylla*, leafless lawyer *Rubus squarrosus*, and a sprawling relative of kōtukutuku, *Fuchsia perscandens*.

Five parasitic mistletoes are found in the Dunedin area, two of which are significant on the peninsula – *Ileostylus micranthus* and the much smaller, easily overlooked *Korthalsella lindsayi*. The former grows on a range of native and introduced species, but coprosmas are a favourite host. Among the ground plants, orchids feature. There are 11 species on the peninsula and they occupy a range of habitats, including forest, rock outcrops and banks. Sandymount is a haven for orchids, including the small yellow-flowered epiphyte *Drymoanthus flavum*, named in 1994.

Certain exotic trees and shrubs have a high profile on the peninsula, notably the Monterey cypress *Cupressus macrocarpa*, shelter belts of which are everywhere to be seen festooned with the native fleshy fern *Pyrrosia eleagnifolia*, and elderberry trees and lupins, both of which spread freely, especially on sandy country. A disease hit the lupin in the late 1980s, causing widespread dieback and leaving many dunelands looking devastated. The disease, affecting the roots, is thought to be cyclical and could cause periodic diebacks in the lupin areas in the years ahead.

Often associated with stands of lupin is a common shrub, poroporo *Solanum laciniatum*, which reaches a height of 3–4m. In summer it bears elegant purple flowers followed by impressive yellow-orange fruit that resemble miniature tamarillos. The fruits often have a hole in them – the exit hole of the moth *Sceliodes cordalis*, whose caterpillar feeds within. Beware the unripe fruits: they are poisonous.

Marram grass *Ammophila arenaria*, an introduced species, now dominates the foredune vegetation – once the preserve of the native orange-leaved sand sedge pīngao *Ficinia spiralis*. Pīngao survives in only a few places, mainly on cliffs where marram grass cannot crowd it out, but several beaches are being replanted with pīngao through projects supported by conservation groups and Māori communities.

ABOVE LEFT: Kōhūhū *Pittosporum tenuifolium* in flower. NP

ABOVE RIGHT: The native tree daisy *Olearia aborescens* produces masses of honey-scented flowers. NP

ABOVE: This flightless caddisfly – the recently described *Pseudoeconesus paludis* – is endemic to Dunedin and common on Otago Peninsula in seepages (such as at Okia Flat) surrounded by *Carex appressa* and other sedges. The only other known locality for it is a seepage at 700m on Swampy Summit. With both sexes flightless, this caddisfly is a strong runner in a habitat where predacious water spiders *Dolomedes minor* abound. BP

PROTECTED AREAS

About 1000ha (10 per cent) of Otago Peninsula land is protected, with most reserves under Department of Conservation management.

The oldest reserve is the Sandfly Bay Wildlife Refuge (338ha), created in 1908. There are now protected areas on either side of it (Sandymount Recreation Reserve and Boulder Beach Conservation Area), and together they make up an 8km coastal strip stretching from Highcliff to Allans Beach. The Yellow-Eyed Penguin Trust in association with the Dunedin City Council manages a 231ha reserve at Okia Flat. The trust also manages a small reserve at Otekiho near Taiaroa.

In 2008, as a result of a highly publicised community initiative, the City Council purchased the Harbour Cone / Hereweka farm property (328ha) to protect its landscape, ecological, recreational, cultural and historical values. The property has iconic landscape features. Pockets of native bush have been enhanced by community planting, and a network of walking routes across the property is marked by yellow-capped poles. Public access is unavailable at lambing time.

Several private landholders have negotiated the placement of covenants over patches of bush on their properties. One example is the Peggys Hill patch, now fenced off from adjacent farmland. The bush here contains a few plants that have disappeared from most other parts of the peninsula, including *Raukaua simplex* (haumakāroa), *Coprosma foetidissima* (hūpiro), and mountain holly or hakeke *Olearia ilicifolia*. Styles Bush at Broad Bay is another notable covenanted area, which has been enhanced by a replanting programme.

The City Council has a few small reserves and it also maintains a network of walking tracks on the peninsula.

OKIA FLAT

On Okia Flat behind the dunes of Victory Beach, the longest (4km) stretch of sand on the Peninsula, coastal turf and duneland plants abound.

Some of these are vulnerable, however. They include sand bidibid *Acaena pallida*, a low stout herb with reddish flowerheads. It is found at only two other sites in New Zealand beyond Otago Peninsula. A close relative, *Acaena novae-zelandiae*, is common.

The diminutive shrub pātōtara *Leucopogon fraseri* forms straggly mats amid the grasses. Its fruits, orange and succulent when ripe, are deliciously sweet. On the foredunes are thickets of New Zealand flax or harakeke *Phormium tenax*. Phormium is from a Greek word for basket and refers to the Māori use of the leaves.

In the back-dune hollows of Okia Flat, an ephemeral wetland flora of rushes and sedges and the short turf areas support a distinctive assemblage of beetles, bugs and moths. Much of the fauna is diurnal, delighting to fly or run on the warmest days. It includes the following moths – the elegant crambid moth *Diasemia grammalis*, the pyralid *Delogenes limodoxa* and the geometrid *Arctesthes catapyrrha*. The larvae of the last mentioned feed here on *Nertera setulosa*.

ABOVE: Clifftop vegetation at Cape Saunders featuring silver tussock *Poa cita*, greenish-orange cushions of *Scleranthus uniflorus* and wind-shorn shrubs of *Melicytus crassifolius*. Also growing here are a variety of *Raoulia* species, compact small cushions of *Colobanthus muelleri* and other native herbs and grasses. BP

CLIFF-DWELLERS

A significant number of Otago Peninsula's rare and special plant species occur on cliffs and coastal banks, no doubt because such habitats are protected by their inaccessibility.

The star turn is a rock daisy that is found nowhere else – *Helichrysum intermedium* var. *tumidum*, the Cape Saunders rock daisy. It clings to cliffs at Cape Saunders and a little further south at Sandymount. Its cylindrical stems, with tiny leaves tightly bound, appear swollen (tumid). A profusion of small, pale yellow flowers (December–January) at the tip of the stems highlights the rounded, compact form of the shrub, which seems secure in its habitat of lichen-encrusted cliffs. It is stouter than *H. intermedium*, which is found inland on rocky sites in the mountains.

Two native forget-me-nots and a native daphne are notable. The white-flowered southern forget-me-not *Myosotis rakiura* was rediscovered at Highcliff in recent years – its northernmost location. It was named after the Māori name for Stewart Island, where it is common. Its diminutive relative, *Myosotis pygmaea* var. *pygmaea*, is found at only a few locations along peninsula clifftops. Both forget-me-nots flower over summer. The daphne relative is the glaucous-leaved *Pimelea carnosa*, possibly a hybrid population restricted to a few clifftops.

Some plants that are common high up in the mountains are established on peninsula cliffs as well, among them the grass tree or inaka *Dracophyllum longifolium* and mat daisies that develop cushion-like form – *Raoulia australis* and *Raoulia beauverdii*.

Common native cliff-dwellers include the ubiquitous iceplant *Disphyma australe*, the yellow-flowering shore groundsel *Senecio carnosulus* (type locality, Black Head), coastal speedwell *Hebe elliptica*, and shore spinach *Tetragonia*

ABOVE: The Cape Saunders rock daisy *Helichrysum intermedium* var. *tumidum*, an Otago Peninsula endemic. NP

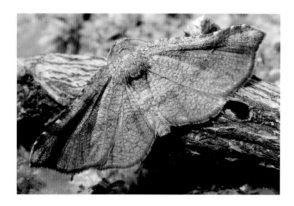

ABOVE: This muehlenbeckia moth *Morova subfasciatus* has just emerged from the small hole on the stem (lower right). The larvae spend their entire lives inside the stems, causing a swelling to form, in which they feed and eventually pupate. An escape route for the emerging adult is made by the caterpillar beforehand and the hole is covered with silk to hide it from the attentions of parasitic flies or wasps. BP

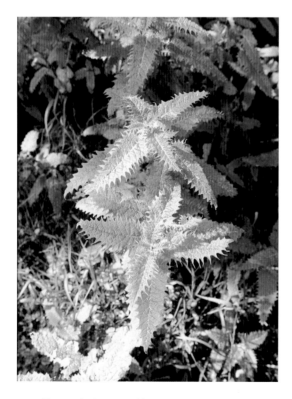

ABOVE: Tree nettle (ongaonga) leaves and white stinging hairs in Sandymount forest. NP

trigyna, which drapes its fleshy leaves over rocks and other plants.

Providing a fluffy cap along the cliffs in many places is the handsome coastal blue tussock *Poa astonii*.

MUEHLENBECKIA | AN IMAGE PROBLEM

Ordinarily confined to the forest edge, *Muehlenbeckia australis* is a scrambling plant that is much maligned for its habit of cloaking remnant shrubland and low regenerating forest. It is often regarded as a smothering weed, but merits a better image for the role it plays as a host to invertebrate fauna, including on Otago Peninsula two copper butterflies and over 20 moth species. Stick insects and beetles are also fond of it.

TWO SIDES TO TREE NETTLE

The tree nettle *Urtica ferox* or ongaonga is a plant to admire but not touch. Its white bristles contain three kinds of poison that will inflict a painful rash if brushed against. People repeatedly stung can become seriously ill. Ongaonga, which grows to about 3m in height, is common on bush margins and disturbed, semi-shaded sites. Watch out for it, especially on track margins at Sandymount and Highcliff.

There is another side to ongaonga, though. It is used by yellow-eyed penguins as a breeding habitat and it is also popular with insects. It is a host plant for the majestic red admiral butterfly, whose fat caterpillars not only feed on the leaves but also mimic the nettle by carrying around their own array of spines. When not feeding, the larvae shelter within a curled leaf and may later pupate there. Other insects attracted to nettle include a leaf-mining fly, two elegant geometrid moths, two noctuid moths and a brown pyraustine moth. The larvae of all of them feed on the foliage – rather carefully!

The much smaller nettle *Urtica incisa*, also native, is another important host for insects, but it is becoming rare now and is confined to a few bush remnants.

COOK'S SCURVY GRASS

Two endemic cress species are now recognised for the Otago coast in a 2013 revision of what was known as Cook's scurvy grass. Both *Lepidium crassum* (the Mole, Aramoana) and *L. juvencum* (Long Beach and Green Island) are endemic to the southeastern South Island and some islands in Foveaux Strait, and are among New Zealand's rarest herbs. Collectively they were used by Captain Cook as a vitamin C supplement in his crew's diet – a remedy for scurvy. Highly palatable to stock and rabbits, they have now become endangered, with *L. juvencum* listed as 'threatened, nationally critical'. For *L. crassum* one of its largest remaining populations is found in an unusual place – the Mole at Aramoana, a man-made structure of rocks which gulls and terns frequent. The plant is known to thrive in coastal locations where seabird droppings (guano) are plentiful.

MARINE CADDISFLY | ODD ONE OUT

Most insects are land-based. Generally, they have left marine habitats to their arthropod relatives, the crustacea. Among the exceptions is the marine caddisfly, a group of five species related to moths and represented in Otago Harbour by one species.

The peninsula caddisfly is *Philanisus plebeius*, a species shared with southeast Australia. The rocky shores between Portobello and Vauxhall support the southernmost population of this species. The other four known species of caddisfly dependent on the sea are endemic to discrete parts of New Zealand.

Adults tend to be active at night, flying around lights during summer evenings. By day they might rest on the undersides of boatsheds. The larvae are quite different. They construct a protective case from silk, decorated with rock-pool plants. This makes them very hard to find in the rock pools around the harbour where they feed on various algae species.

Caddisfly species associated with fresh water are prolific on Otago Peninsula, where some 15 species are recorded, some flightless, others diurnal.

ABOVE: The newly described crucifer *Lepidium juvencum* in flower on Green Island. Related to the common cabbage, it thrives in a guano environment close to the sea and is a host plant for the introduced diamond-back moth and white butterfly. NP

ABOVE: Adult and larval case (TOP) of marine caddisfly *Philanisus plebeius* in an Otago Harbour rock pool. Its black head protrudes from the case, which is about 15mm long. BP

SCORPIONFLIES AND STONEFLIES

The insect order Mecoptera (scorpionflies) has only one New Zealand representative, *Nannochorista philpotti*. It is common on Otago Peninsula, where its elongate larvae feed in the mud of slow-moving streams.

In common with stoneflies, mayflies and caddisflies, the scorpionfly depends on fresh water for larval growth. But the adults of all these groups shun the aquatic life, preferring to live in streamside vegetation or on rocks.

Stoneflies, although fully winged, characteristically prefer to walk rather than fly. No fewer than 10 species of stonefly have been recorded from the peninsula. The commonest include a long-winged brown lowland variety of *Zelandobius foxi* and its fast-moving congener, *Z. uniramus*.

JEWELLED GECKO

The brilliantly coloured jewelled gecko or mokokākāriki *Naultinus gemmeus*, a species of green tree gecko found only in the South Island, is one of Otago Peninsula's rarer inhabitants.

Reaching 18cm in length, this gecko lives in shrubland, typically on bushes of twiggy, small-leaved *Coprosma propinqua*. Using its tail to hold on, it will drape itself over outer branches on sunny days, waiting to catch passing insects. Young are born live in early winter, usually two at a time.

Like New Zealand's seven other species of diurnal tree gecko, the jewelled gecko is well camouflaged. It is predominantly green, with yellow or white stripes running lengthwise, often interspersed with diamond-shaped splotches.

The species is found east of the main divide between Banks Peninsula and Nugget Point, with Otago Peninsula a stronghold for it. Small populations occur at more than 20 places on the peninsula.

Efforts to protect the jewelled gecko from introduced mammalian predators, such as feral cats, rats, mice, stoats and weasels, include community trapping projects and planting to extend their habitat. To assist the species there have been several translocations into Orokonui Ecosanctuary. A greater threat than predation has been poaching of the geckos for markets in Europe. Several poachers from overseas have been convicted in New Zealand courts but the threat remains.

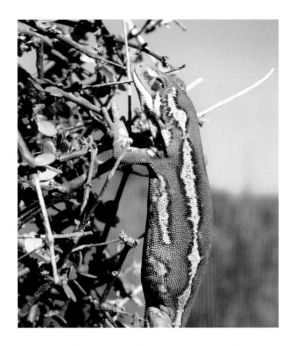

ABOVE: A jewelled gecko climbing on a coprosma bush.
Carey Knox

BELOW, FAR LEFT: A jewelled gecko, marked with blue spots by scientists studying its movements, basks on a *Coprosma propinqua* shrub. NP
CENTRE: Jewelled geckos display spectacular patterns. Carey Knox
BELOW: The colourful head of a jewelled gecko. Carey Knox

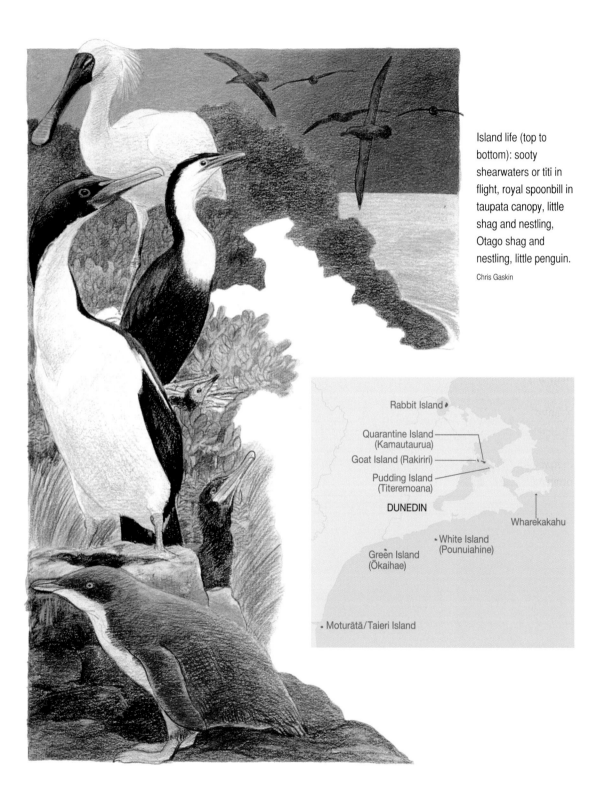

Island life (top to bottom): sooty shearwaters or tītī in flight, royal spoonbill in taupata canopy, little shag and nestling, Otago shag and nestling, little penguin.

Chris Gaskin

Rabbit Island

Quarantine Island (Kamautaurua)

Goat Island (Rakiriri)

Pudding Island (Titeremoana)

DUNEDIN

Wharekakahu

White Island (Pounuiahine)

Green Island (Ōkaihae)

Moturātā/Taieri Island

ABOVE: Green Island from the southern side, with Kaikorai Estuary in the distance. NP

ISLANDS are intriguing places. They conjure up thoughts of remoteness, tranquillity and nature unspoiled. Most people – certainly those for whom wilderness is a tonic – feel compelled to explore islands where they can. Around Dunedin, however, the opportunities are few. There are as many islands of note in Lake Wanaka alone as there are along the coastline from Waikouaiti to Taieri Mouth.

Nonetheless, each of the Dunedin islands retains unique natural or conservation values of one kind or another. In common with other New Zealand regions, Dunedin has islands that are important havens for rare or special fauna and flora.

The offshore islands are Green Island or Ōkaihae off the Waldronville coast, White Island or Pounuiahine off St Clair Beach, and Wharekakahu, which lies between Cape Saunders and Allans Beach. Taieri Island or Moturātā, guarding the mouth of the Taieri River, can be reached on foot at low tide. White Island and the Gull Rocks off Sandfly Bay are too small, low-lying and wave-swept to retain significant natural values.

ABOVE: *Hebe elliptica*, a coastal shrub. Flowers are white or sometimes mauve. NP

ABOVE RIGHT: The pinkish-purple larvae of the geometrid moth *Pasiphila charybdis* feed on the leaves of *Hebe elliptica*. Dunedin is the type locality for this moth species, whose close relative *P. fumipalpata* feeds on the flowers of the same shrub, which supports many insects. BP

Otago Harbour has two 'halfway' islands: Quarantine Island or Kamautaurua (also known as St Martin Island) and Goat Island or Rangiriri, which all but span the gap between Port Chalmers and Portobello Peninsula. Nearer Portobello village is tiny circular Pudding Island or Titeremoana, a scenic reserve entirely covered in low forest to the cliff edge, in the way the harbour shores were clothed in pre-European times.

Finally, and in a different category again, is Rabbit Island, which stands out – just – above the tidal flats of Blueskin Bay.

GREEN ISLAND | TREASURE ISLAND

Volcanic Green Island, 4.5ha in extent, 42m high and 2.2km from the mainland, is a natural treasure. A nature reserve (closed to the public; landings by permit only), it is chock-a-block with seabirds.

The little penguin population alone is impressive, although it fluctuates a lot. Nest counts can range from 100 to 1500, depending on factors such as food supply. Yellow-eyed penguins are rather more consistent – 25–30 pairs. Stewart Island shags nest in a tight colony on open ground on the north face (100–200 nests), and royal spoonbills or kōtuku-ngutupapa arrived in 1988 to establish a colony of about 30 nests in the canopy of the predominant shrub, taupata *Coprosma repens*. Little shags also nest in the canopy.

Fairy prions or tītīwainui, a small blue-grey petrel about half the size of the sooty shearwater, are abundant (in the order of 1000 nests). They nest in burrows, on crevices or in caves. They also have a small colony on the sandstone cliffs near Tunnel Beach, which suggests they might have nested in greater numbers on the mainland in the past, but succumbed to predators. These prions breed on offshore islands in many parts of New Zealand, as well as on numerous subantarctic islands around the Southern Ocean.

Southern black-backed gulls also inhabit Green Island. Their nests number about 200 each year. Only a handful of sooty shearwaters nest here, though. Variable (black) oystercatchers – two or three pairs – breed on the island, nesting close to the water.

ABOVE: Royal spoonbill nests on Green Island, with an early chick occupying one and eggs in another. NP

ROYAL NEWCOMERS

Royal spoonbills or kōtuku-ngutupapa *Platalea regia* nest in bushes of taupata *Coprosma repens* on Green Island. Breeding was confirmed in 1988, and by 1995 the colony had up to 25 nests. There is a colony at Maukiekie Island off Moeraki Peninsula in North Otago, established in 1984, and another at Taieri Island or Moturātā, off Taieri Mouth. The fourth Otago colony – the first on the South Island east coast – is at Taiaroa Head.

Royal spoonbills also breed near Okarito Lagoon and at Wairau Lagoon in Marlborough. Although the Otago colonies are younger, Otago is now a main region for royal spoonbills. It is not unusual for annual census counts to record over 200 birds on the Otago coast.

Like the distantly related white heron or kōtuku, royal spoonbills are self-introduced from Australia. They feed on tidal mudflats in a distinctive way, sweeping their extraordinary jet-black spoon-shaped bills from side to side in search of small fish and estuarine crustaceans, molluscs and worms.

Kaikorai Estuary is a favourite haunt, and they are often seen from the bridge on Brighton Road. They can appear at any of the Dunedin estuaries and even on the mudflats and soft shores of Otago Harbour. At Green Island the breeding season begins in October, with the return of the birds from winter quarters in northern areas of New Zealand. Nests are built of sticks and leaves and one to four eggs are laid. The chicks fledge in about seven weeks, after which they follow and are fed by their parents for a few weeks.

One of the most remarkable features of the birdlife of Green Island involves an introduced species – the starling. In their thousands, starlings flock to the island from the mainland on a daily basis, around dusk, to roost in the taupata canopy overnight. Only a few breed there, however.

There is a population of a large Otago gecko, *Woodworthia new species*, and small numbers of common gecko *Heterophilus maculatus* on Green Island.

Shrubland covers about 40 per cent of the island, the rest being rocky or covered in herbs or bird droppings. The guano inhibits all but a few plants.

Green Island has a small flora compared to the harbour islands – just eight native species and ten naturalised ones. Taupata, a native shrub, dominates the scene. Its shiny foliage forms virtually the whole canopy, which reaches about 4m in height in sheltered places but is characteristically 1–2m. The only other shrub species here is *Hebe elliptica*, which once predominated. There are only a few hebe trees left now. Since about 1960 the hebe has been all but displaced by taupata – an astonishing transformation. Underneath the taupata, the ground is largely bare except for leaf litter.

Taupata proliferates on the Dunedin coastline, although its natural southern limit is thought to be Kaikoura. It was brought south as a hedging plant, conspicuous at Brighton, from where starlings and other birds probably carried the seed to Green Island. In Australia taupata is known as New Zealand mirror bush and regarded as a weed.

A handful of plants of the rare and endangered cress *Lepidium juvencum*, in the Cook's scurvy grass group, grow on the south side of the island on two sites. Muddy terraces on the west side are covered by mats of the fleshy herb *Crassula moschata* and the common introduced grass *Poa annua*. Exotic plant species on Green Island include the tall tree mallow *Lavatera arborea*, which is being controlled.

MOTURĀTĀ | TĪTĪ TERRITORY

Moturātā or Taieri Island (an elongate 6.8ha, 31m at its highest point) is joined to the mainland by a sand bar that is covered at high tide. As a result of a history of human occupation and use – initially by local Māori, then by European whalers – its vegetation is much modified.

Flax *Phormium tenax* dominates. Other notable native species are bracken *Pteridium esculentum*, silver tussock *Poa cita* and poroporo *Solanum laciniatum*. Native celery *Apium prostratum*, not unlike flat-leaved parsley in appearance, grows just above the high-tide mark. Like the cress *Lepidium juvencum*, it was used by Captain Cook to ward off scurvy. Gorse and thistles are scattered across the island's grassy slopes.

A revegetation programme involving members of the Moturātā–Taieri Mouth Whānau and other residents, working in conjunction with the Department of Conservation, has restored shrubland on northern parts of the island. Rabbits have inhabited the island in the past and will be a threat to regeneration if not controlled.

ABOVE: Sooty shearwater or tītī *Puffinus griseus* feeding off the Otago coast.

Stephen Jaquiery / *Otago Daily Times*

Rabbits in number would compete for burrowing space with tītī (sooty shearwaters), whose presence on the island is of significance to Māori people. Harvesting of tītī chicks as muttonbirds is still a traditional practice of southern Māori on islands around Stewart Island, but it is not permitted on Moturātā, a scenic reserve. In spring, tītī migrate south in their millions from winter quarters in the North Pacific. Huge flocks work their way south along the Dunedin coast. They crowd onto islands in southern New Zealand, especially in the Stewart Island and Foveaux Strait area and at The Snares, raising a single chick per pair over summer. Smaller colonies are located on the mainland and on islands such as Green and Moturātā. The chicks are ready to fledge in April–May, after which they join the adults in the long migration flight north.

The island's name, literally Rātā Island, may reflect the presence of southern rātā *Metrosideros umbellata* at one time. Rātā does not occur naturally in the Dunedin area. It extends north along the coast from South Otago as far as Akatore, close to Taieri Mouth. Its absence north of here is a mystery.

ABOVE: The island of Wharekakahu off Cape Saunders, as viewed from the Sandymount area. NP

FAR RIGHT: Wind-shorn shrubs and trees on the south side of Quarantine Island – peppertree (foreground), small-leaved coprosma species hosting the mistletoe *Ileostylus micranthus*, and Hall's tōtara. NP

WHAREKAKAHU

Cliff-bound Wharekakahu Island (2.1ha, 52m high), a nature reserve off-limits to the public, is separated from the Otago Peninsula coastline by about 300m of often stormy ocean. Cape Saunders lighthouse is about 1km away. As on Green Island, fairy prions and Otago shags breed in number here, with about 200 shag nests. Spotted shags nest in smaller numbers on the cliff ledges. Red-billed gulls also have a colony. The green skink *Oligosoma chloronoton*, an Otago endemic that reaches a length of 20cm, has been recorded on the island. Increasing colonisation by the Otago shags has reduced plant species formerly abundant on the island, notably the shrub *Hebe elliptica* and small blue tussock *Poa astonii*.

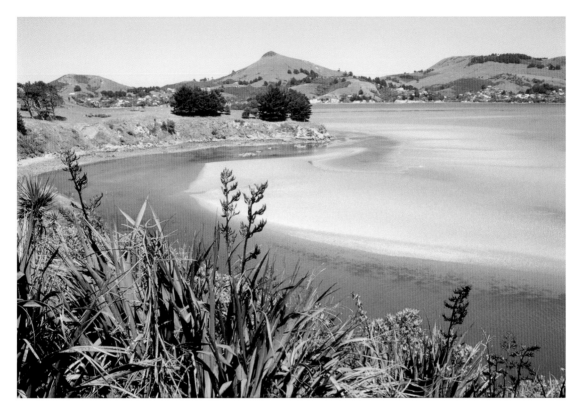

ABOVE: Flax flowers (January) rise above mixed shrubland on the southwest side of Quarantine Island. In the distance is Harbour Cone. NP

QUARANTINE ISLAND AND GOAT ISLAND | SPECIES RICH

The two islands that divide Otago Harbour into upper and lower compartments – Quarantine or Kamautaurua and Goat or Rangiriri – retain a diverse array of plant life, with each island boasting about 100 native species.

On Quarantine Island (14ha, 58m above sea level at the summit), dense native forest covers western areas, which are fenced off from pasture grazed by sheep. Hall's tōtara, māhoe, broadleaf, ngaio and kōhūhū make up the bulk of the canopy. What impresses in this low forest is the proliferation of climbing plants or lianes – 11 species all told. They add complexity to the forest. It becomes a jungle.

With no possums on the island to eat their leaves and flowers, the lianes can scramble at will.

MICRO-CASEMOTHS

Three species of micro-casemoth are found on the islands and coast of Dunedin. Pictured left is the male of one of two undescribed *Reductoderces* species, which reaches its northern limit on Otago Peninsula and its islands. Wingless females cling to their cases after emerging on calm frosty mornings in July–August, then release a distinctive scent (pheromone) to attract a mate. They lay their eggs back in the empty case. The cases are small but can occur in very large numbers. The larvae carry around the case for shelter and camouflage as they feed on various algae species. The third species *Scoriodyta patricki* is found from Oamaru south to Otago Peninsula, with Portobello being the type locality. BP

NIGHT MOTH

The winter noctuid moth *Agrotis* aff. *innominata* has larvae feeding on both marram grass and sand convolvulus *Calystegia soldanella*. While the males are strong fliers between June and August, the females in southern New Zealand populations are short-winged (brachypterous) and consequently flightless, which greatly limits the dispersal ability of the species. Pictured left is the flightless adult female. BP

RED KATIPŌ

The red katipō spider *Latrodectus katipo*, which lives exclusively in sandy areas and always near the sea, is at its southern limit at Doctors Point, although the species is more common at Karitane Beach, especially where marram grass is not too dense. The only poisonous animal native to New Zealand, it belongs to a group of poisonous spiders found in many parts of the world.

Only the female is able to bite. She is shiny black with a red-striped abdomen the size of a garden pea, and like many other spiders, she guards her egg sac to prevent other creatures, notably carnivorous beetles, from eating them. Females may live 18 to 24 months but males are short-lived (5 to 6 weeks). The male is quite different. It is much smaller with a white abdomen that carries black bands and light red or orange diamonds.

Shy spiders, red katipō are far less dangerous than their reputation suggests. Sometimes they are caught up in driftwood collected from the beach. They live in marram grass and other seashore vegetation, though they may shelter under empty cans or other rubbish. Their Māori name means 'night biter'.

ABOVE: A female katipō spider. BP

Climbing anise *Scandia geniculata*, which is palatable to stock and now fairly rare in the Dunedin area, is well established on Quarantine Island. So too is the native bindweed *Calystegia tuguriorum*, which is similar to garden convolvulus but with smaller flowers (up to 5cm diameter) and distinctive orange seeds. White-flowered climbing rātā *Metrosideros diffusa* and the native jasmine or kaihua *Parsonsia heterophylla* are abundant. Ferns dominate the ground cover.

The forest is in much better condition overall than similar forest on adjacent Otago Peninsula. The island, separated from the Peninsula by a 100m-wide channel swept by tidal currents, is free not only of possums but also of rabbits, cats, mice, stoats and ferrets – good news for the bellbird, grey warbler, rifleman (reintroduced) and other bush birds. Rats are present but under control. Southern black-backed gulls nest on grassy slopes close to the water and little shags build their nests in trees at the water's edge or overhanging it.

Sheep have grazed the island for decades but numbers have reduced to a 'lawnmower' flock. At the same time, planting out of native trees and shrubs by the Conservation Corps, Kiwi Conservation Club (Forest & Bird), Dunedin Amenities Society and St Martin Island Community has assisted natural revegetation.

In summer, the air around the forest margins is alive with butterflies – red admiral, tussock and two copper species (common and glade).

Quarantine Island is a recreation reserve managed by the Department of Conservation and leased to the St Martin Island Community. Visitors are welcome. From 1863 to the 1920s, the island was a quarantine station. Passengers from 41 immigrant vessels were quarantined there. A cemetery surrounded by a relatively new picket fence recalls the fact that some 72 immigrants died of diseases. The introduced conifers, including Scots pine around the cemetery, date from the quarantine station era. World War I soldiers suffering venereal disease were housed in the island's hospital, and in 1928, huskies with Rear Admiral Richard Evelyn Byrd's Antarctic expedition were quarantined on the island. Lacking fresh water, the island was never the site of major settlement by early Māori.

The main shipping channel separates Quarantine Island from Goat Island or Rangiriri, a scenic reserve (4.6ha, 40m above sea level), where regenerating low forest covers virtually the whole island. Cleared of its original forest in the 1870s for quarantine purposes, Goat Island now bears an outstanding example of the ngaio–kōhūhū association. Cabbage trees *Cordyline australis* (tī), tōtara and an occasional miro are emergent. In addition to having most of the climbing plants found on Quarantine, Goat Island has supplejack or kareao *Ripogonum scandens*. It, too, is free of introduced browsing animals.

TITEREMOANA RESTORED

Titeremoana (0.8ha) is a scenic reserve which can be reached on foot at low tide. In December 1909, careless visitors caused a fire which partly destroyed the indigenous vegetation. The following year the island was declared a reserve and replanted by the Forest Service with 900 seedlings of native shrubs and trees. This accounts for the presence on the island of some odd trees, including akiraho *Olearia*

RIGHT: A southern black-backed gull chick close to its nest on a rock stack beside Pudding Island / Titeremoana, near Portobello. The island is fully covered by a dense forest of ngaio, kōhūhū, broadleaf and tōtara that reaches a surprising height – 7m. NP

RIGHT: This white-fronted tern was defending a nest site below iceplant flowers on the cliffs of Pudding Island. NP

RIGHT: Rabbit Island inhabitant: *Coprosma acerosa* fruiting.

Peter Johnson

paniculata, which does not occur naturally south of Oamaru but is common as a hedging species around Dunedin, and silver beech or tawhai *Lophozonia menziesii*, rare at sea level in the Dunedin region. Three trees of pōhutukawa *Metrosideros excelsa*, which grow on the eastern side of the island, probably date from this early exercise in habitat restoration. They flower in January–February, which is later than their northern equivalent. Today the understorey over much of the island is relatively open, with hound's tongue fern *Phymatosorus diversifolius* and tangled native jasmine providing a fairly complete ground cover.

RABBIT ISLAND | LOW PROFILE

Rabbit Island, about 1km long and rising only a few metres above sea level, is surrounded by the saltmarsh of Blueskin Bay. The saltmarsh (see Chapter 5) has not been disturbed much, but vegetation on the island proper has suffered by the invasion of gorse, broom and *Pinus radiata*. Mānuka *Leptospermum scoparium* is holding its own, however, at the north and south ends of the island, with some trees growing to 6m. The sand coprosma *Coprosma acerosa* has been recorded on the island. Reaching 2m, it produces translucent pale-blue fruit in late summer.

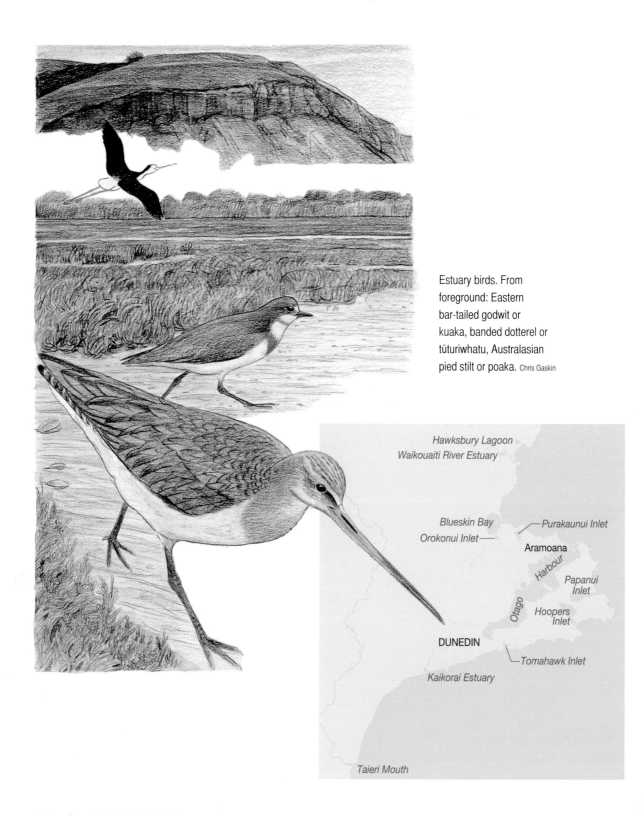

Estuary birds. From foreground: Eastern bar-tailed godwit or kuaka, banded dotterel or tūturiwhatu, Australasian pied stilt or poaka. Chris Gaskin

Hawksbury Lagoon
Waikouaiti River Estuary

Blueskin Bay
Orokonui Inlet——

——Purakaunui Inlet

Aramoana

Papanui Inlet

Hoopers Inlet

Otago Harbour

DUNEDIN

——Tomahawk Inlet

Kaikorai Estuary

Taieri Mouth

CHAPTER **5** | # ESTUARIES, INLETS & LAGOONS
CARESSED BY THE TIDE

ISLANDS STAND FAST against the tide; estuaries, inlets and lagoons have a rather more accommodating relationship with the sea. Caressed by tides twice a day, they are among the most dynamic places in nature. Long before dinosaurs ruled the earth, marine fauna with terrestrial ambitions slithered ashore in the shelter and repose of estuaries – and gained a foothold. Among the habitats of the modern world, estuaries remain the creative engine rooms of nature they once were. For an object lesson in the rhythms and interconnectedness of nature, look no further than an estuary.

What Dunedin lacks in the way of islands it makes up for in tidal inlets, estuaries and lagoons. The list includes (from north to south) Hawksbury Lagoon, Waikouaiti River Estuary at Karitane/Merton, Blueskin Bay and Orokonui Inlets, Purakaunui Inlet, Aramoana, Hoopers and Papanui Inlets on Otago Peninsula, Tomahawk Lagoon, Kaikorai Estuary and Lagoon, and Taieri Mouth. Estuaries are typically river mouths defined by a sand spit behind which the tide covers and uncovers an expanse of mudflats and saltmarsh. Strictly speaking, Otago Harbour is an inlet; but it resembles a broad river in shape, complete with a sand spit that protects a splendid estuary – Aramoana.

Saltmarsh can be divided into zones (commonly upper, middle and lower), with the size and make-up of each zone determined by the extent to which it is immersed and exposed by the tide and the degree of salinity in the sandy soils. The upper marsh is flooded only at spring tides, which occur with each full and new moon. Behind the marsh there are often sand ridges and wet slacks, which together act as a giant filter. Freshwater run-off is intercepted and mixed gradually with the brine, providing plants with some assurance of salinity levels. As sea levels rise and fall over eons, the saltmarsh migrates, retaining its pattern of zonation.

The productivity of estuaries – the intertidal flats and saltmarsh – is astonishing. New Zealand studies suggest estuaries may produce as much as 2kg of plant matter per square metre each year (compared with 730g for land and 155g for the ocean). At least 30 commercially important fish species, including flounder, mullet, sole, gurnard, red cod, eels and whitebait, migrate through estuaries.

This huge productivity is possible because, twice a day, the tide freshens the nutrient supply. For the microorganisms, plants, shellfish, crustaceans, fish and birds it is a regular, moving feast. The tide also brings in sediment, which shifts about, building here, eroding there, steadily redefining the shape of things in an estuary.

Some 800,000 tonnes of sediment pour into Otago Harbour over the course of each year. Some of this exits with the ebb tide, but much of it settles. Without dredging (and if sea levels remained the same), the harbour would fill up in about 150 years. At low tide about 30 per cent of the harbour (4600ha) is exposed as flats. It takes only two tides to turn over water in the lower harbour but 27 tides (just on two weeks) for a complete turnover to be achieved in the upper harbour, separated from the lower compartment by the two islands near Port Chalmers.

CATALOGUE OF MISUSE

In Dunedin, as elsewhere in New Zealand, estuaries and the shallows of inlets and lagoons used to be regarded by Europeans as being muddy eyesores – wastelands in limbo, of value only when reclaimed and put to human use.

The poor image of estuaries is no better expressed than in the siting of public rubbish dumps on many of them – a crude and contaminating form of reclamation. There have been other uses, including plantation forestry, sports grounds, causeway roading and subdivisions. Only in recent times has the ecological importance of estuaries been recognised – for example, their role as nursery areas for fish and as sources of enrichment for coastal waters.

Reclamation has a habit of creeping up on and severely modifying an estuarine ecosystem. In Otago Harbour, the total area reclaimed since 1847 is now close to 400ha – 8 per cent of the original area at high water. The upper harbour is practically devoid of estuarine habitat. An area of about 25ha centred on Logan Park was once a sizeable wetland – Lake Logan. Much of the commercial and industrial sector of downtown Dunedin occupies reclaimed mudflats and saltmarsh.

The estuary of the Waikouaiti River had by far the greatest area of pre-European saltmarsh in Otago. The bulk of it was drained for farmland.

PROBLEM PLANTS

An Asian seaweed *Undaria pinnatifida*, which thrives in sheltered waters, is becoming a threat to native marine plants. It was discovered at Port Chalmers and the Dunedin Steamer Basin in 1990. Introduced accidentally with water ballast discharged by overseas ships, *Undaria* may locally displace the ubiquitous native bladder kelp *Macrocystis pyrifera* if left unchecked. In Asia, the seaweed is farmed as wakame.

The cord grass *Spartina anglica*, introduced from Britain to assist reclamation of estuaries, is capable of destroying native saltmarsh vegetation if not kept in check. It is an aggressive plant, forming stout clumps to knee height and spreading rhizomes through tidal mud. By trapping sediments it can elevate a tidal zone. Spartina had a foothold at Merton near Cherry Farm in the 1980s, but has been controlled by a spraying programme undertaken by the Department of Conservation.

ABOVE: Purakaunui Inlet lies east of Blueskin Bay. NP

RARE TREE

At Heyward Point north of Aramoana is a relict group of the small native tree daisy *Olearia hectorii*, discovered in the late 1990s growing on private land. A threatened species up to 8m tall, it survives in small disjunct patches across both the South and North Islands. The nearest population to this east Otago location is the Owaka Valley in South Otago. There is also a group in the Matukituki Valley west of Wanaka.

ABOVE: Glasswort *Sarcocornia quinqueflora* at Aramoana, with saltmarsh ribbonwood in the background. Glasswort also grows on hard shores and cliffs near the sea. Its common name relates to the use of the plant's mineral-rich ash in an old glassmaking process. Caterpillars thrive on this plant, notably those of the moth *Ectopatria aspera*, which are initially green and closely resemble the foliage of glasswort. When the caterpillars become too large to be camouflaged effectively, they turn brown and grey, with rows of white spots dorsally, and hide among the stems and litter at the base of the plant. NP

ARAMOANA | SHOWPIECE SALTMARSH

The saltmarsh tucked in behind Aramoana Spit is the largest and most intact saltmarsh in the Dunedin region and one of the best examples left on the South Island's east coast.

Aramoana saltmarsh is now fully protected within the network of reserves managed by the Department of Conservation, but for many years it was threatened by industrial development. In 1972, the Aramoana saltmarsh and mudflats were earmarked as the site of an aluminium smelter, and in 1981 a second and much larger proposal was mooted – similar in size to Southland's Tiwai Point plant.

A vociferous public campaign opposed the scheme, which was eventually abandoned as uneconomic. The Department of Conservation now manages 120ha of saltmarsh and an adjacent buffer zone as an ecological area. A further 250ha of intertidal flats is also protected.

LEFT: At Aramoana, saltmarsh ribbonwood *Plagianthus divaricatus* forms along the boundary between the tidal saltmarsh and a slightly drier yet still salty zone of saltmarsh meadow. NP

TOP: *Selliera radicans* or remuremu in flower, Otago Harbour. NP

ABOVE: Climbing glasswort frames a flowering example of sea pimpernel *Samolus repens*. NP

The saltmarsh contains a representative suite of plants. Some enjoy a dip in the sea on a daily basis and some only occasionally. Others are shy of the water but accept a shake of salt around their roots. Here the tidal range at mean springs is 1.65m (at Dunedin, 22km from here, the range is 1.8m).

Saltmarsh plants that withstand regular submergence at high tide are a select group. They include glasswort *Sarcocornia quinqueflora*, a succulent whose jointed stems form dense mats. The stems range in colour from reddish brown to blue-green. The sedge three-square *Schoenoplectus pungens*, which grows in open clumps, is also to be found at the reception centre for the incoming tide. It is an old salt of the plant world, having crossed many seas to establish in Europe and North and South America as well as in Australia and New Zealand.

In the middle marsh, submerged for less time, are turf-forming remuremu *Selliera radicans* and shore pimpernel or maakoako *Samolus repens*. They look alike, these two ground-huggers, but their flowers are distinguishing. Samolus bears white stars; selliera's white flowers seem lopsided, with a petal or two missing. Both plants are also found in Australia, and maakoako's range extends to Easter Island. Associated plants in the middle zone are *Suaeda novae-zelandiae*, a reddish endemic sea blite, and the purple-flowered saltmarsh musk *Mimulus repens*. Other distinctive marsh species are bachelor's button *Cotula coronopifolia*, whose yellow flowers are bright as the proverbial button, and *Lilaeopsis novae-zelandiae*, a South Island endemic (type locality, Tomahawk Lagoon) whose cylindrical leaves arise from creeping rhizomes. These and other plants form meadows whose upper boundary is marked by plants of distinctly higher stature.

In the upper saltmarsh are found tall rushes and sedges. Prominent is jointed wire rush or oioi *Apodasmia similis*, which grows in dense stands to over 1m tall with foliage delicately and diversely coloured – blue-green, grey, orange, purple. Often associated with jointed wire rush is saltmarsh ribbonwood *Plagianthus divaricatus* – reaching over 2m, the only shrub to tolerate the saline conditions of the upper saltmarsh and one of New Zealand's few native deciduous species. At Aramoana and other places, the ribbonwood associates with New Zealand flax or harakeke *Phormium tenax*.

From the saltmarsh ribbonwood to the remuremu, marsh plants provide food for over 80 native moth species. Other notable insects include several native staphylinid beetles and a large native chafer, the sand scarab *Pericoptus truncatus*, which is found in the dunes adjacent to the marsh. The jointed wire rush / saltmarsh ribbonwood area is habitat, too, for fernbird *Bowdleria punctata*, a vulnerable native species.

The sand ridges extending inland, reaching 7m above mean sea level, probably originated between 4000 and 6000 years ago, when sea levels were about 2m above present levels.

Since the erection of the Mole (official name, Cargill Pier) in the 1880s, the Spit has been seriously eroded. It used to be much broader. About 12ha has been lost. The saltmarsh, however, owes much to the erection of the Mole, because it extinguished a second channel to the sea and allowed the sandy flats once occupying the site to be invaded by saltmarsh vegetation.

Fringing the Aramoana saltmarsh on the harbour side are intertidal flats that extend for 3km from the end of the Spit to Otafelo Point. Snails and crabs mark the exposed shiny mud with wiggly lines, and the thin dark leaves of seagrass or eelgrass *Zostera novazelandica*, erect and waving when covered in water, lie as if exhausted when the tide is out.

On flats clear of vegetation the most common shellfish is the New Zealand cockle or tuaki *Austrovenus stutchburyi* (more properly a clam but called a cockle by Captain Cook, who thought them the same as Thames Estuary cockles). Filter feeders, cockles achieve an unbelievable density at stable sites where the supply of planktonic food is at an optimum. In tightly packed beds, they can number in the order of several thousand per square metre. A total weight of over 30kg per square metre has been recorded. Such is their number, dead cockle shells wash ashore to cover beaches.

Other molluscs roam the intertidal area. Topshells rasp microscopic algae from zostera leaves. Whelks are carnivorous. They prey on cockles and other shellfish by boring directly through the shell. Unrelated to bivalves such as cockles are two species of brachiopods – shellfish of ancient lineage. In all, 400 species of seabed invertebrate animals have been recorded from Otago Harbour.

Ninety species of fish are known from the harbour, with the Aramoana area playing a key role as a juvenile rearing habitat.

Little wonder, then, that at low tide the mudflats and nearby shallow waters throng with seabirds and wading birds that come to prey on shellfish, finfish, crustaceans and worms. Pied oystercatchers, banded dotterels and red-billed and southern black-backed gulls all take part in the feast, and in the summer they are joined by migratory birds, notably eastern bar-tailed godwits. The waders include white-faced herons, pied stilts, royal spoonbills and on occasion, white herons.

Most birds follow the edge of the ebbing tide, exploring the flats on foot as they become exposed. Black swans, which graze the seagrass, operate the other way. They would rather float than waddle on foot to reach the seagrass, so they swim with the flood tide, dipping their long necks to pull at the grass under water.

The droppings of all these birds contribute substantially to the nutrient soup of the intertidal flats and saltmarsh.

SUPERLATIVE KELP

Bladder kelp *Macrocystis pyrifera*, distinguished by its floats or bladders and ribbon-like form, is common in sheltered waters. Although mainly a subtidal seaweed growing up to 20m long, it is sometimes seen bunched up in the shallows at low tide. In deeper water its upper leaves collect at the surface, forming a brown belt parallel to the shore. Bladder kelp is reputed to be the world's fastest-growing plant. Leaves can put on half a metre a day. In California it is harvested as a source of algin by barges that mow the top 2m at each harvest.

The bulkiest New Zealand seaweed, inhabiting rocky shores where it can gain an anchorage, bull kelp produces fronds up to 10m long and 1m wide near the base. The holdfasts (yellowish stems) anchoring individual plants are undermined by shellfish and worms, which may eventually cause the plant to break away and wash ashore.

A closely related kelp, *Durvillaea willana*, grows to 5m and is distinguished by its more tree-like form. Its blades lack the internal buoyant honeycomb tissue of *D. antarctica*. It is generally located below the zone of bull kelp and is not attacked by burrowing animals.

Sea tulips, attached by stalks up to 1m long, belong to an order of marine animals called acidians or sea squirts. They feed by taking in water through siphons. Sea tulips *Pyura pachydermatina* are plentiful along rocky shores of Otago Harbour and the adjacent coast.

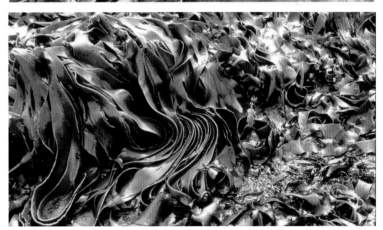

TOP: Giant seaweed: Bull kelp *Durvillaea antarctica* swirls below its anchor points – wave-washed rocks near the entrance to Otago Harbour. NP

CENTRE: Bladder kelp *Macrocystis pyrifera* thrives on rocky shores that are sheltered from waves. NP

BOTTOM: Bull kelp *Durvillaea antarctica* with pink sea tulips, an intertidal animal, in a rock pool at Murdering Beach or Whareakeake. NP

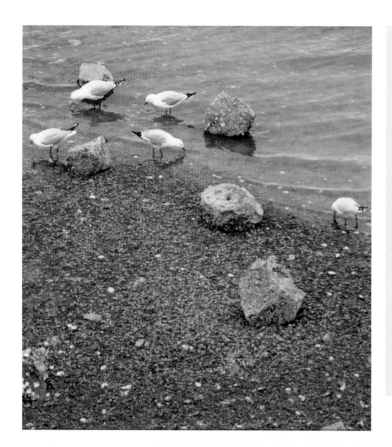

TIDAL MEADOWS

Seagrass *Zostera novazelandica*, spending half its life submerged, is more than a food for black swans and vegetarian shellfish. It creates microhabitats amongst its dense roots and leaves. It also traps sand and shell gravel and forms habitat for juvenile fish.

Seagrass will establish only where the salinity is not too low and where the intertidal flats are gently graded. The tidal current cannot be too strong or the plant will scour out; nor can it be too weak or it will become smothered in silt. Its tiny flowers are fertilised under water and rarely seen.

The roots go deep into the rich black mud that typically underlies seagrass – mud enriched by generations of decaying organisms and plants, including seagrass itself. Seagrass is an important source of phosphorus in the estuarine system.

ABOVE: Red-billed gulls feeding on a stranding of red lobster krill *Munida gregaria* at Portobello. In summer, dense swarms enter the harbour and strand on beaches right up to the head of the harbour. They provide easy picking for gulls, either in the water or on beaches uncovered by the tide. *Munida* is a galatheid crab and the krill, known as whalefood, a postlarval form. 'White krill' *Nyctiphanes australis* is also seasonally conspicuous in the harbour. NP

HAWKSBURY LAGOON | BLACK SWANS

Hawksbury Lagoon at Waikouaiti is a 61ha wildlife management reserve and a haven for aquatic birds. Its reserve status dates from 1900, when it was recognised as an important refuge for 'native and imported game'. Shooting is not permitted. Public access is maintained.

The population of black swans *Cygnus atratus* has been a hallmark of the area in the past. In 1993, however, the population crashed from 300–400 to just 10 – a phenomenon that was linked to an algal bloom in the shallow waters of the lagoon, caused by nutrient enrichment or eutrophication. The reduced transparency resulted in a marked decline in the bottom-dwelling algae upon which the swans fed, and thus the swans moved away. Something similar happened in 1985.

Black swans are no longer regarded as an introduced species per se. Numbers of them were imported from Australia in the 1860s as a game bird and liberated in Otago as well as other parts of the South Island, but no one could account for the population suddenly swelling in the 1960s. Today ornithologists accept there must have been self-introductions then and at later periods.

Black swans do not breed every year. No more than a third of birds in a breeding area in any one year will attempt to nest. Usually five or six eggs are incubated, and within 24 hours of hatching, the cygnets are led to water. Before their breeding years young swans may fly to other regions – the Otago coast sometimes receives visits from Canterbury birds. Black swans are vegetarians, eating mainly aquatic plants.

ABOVE: Hawksbury Lagoon at Waikouaiti is a haven for aquatic birds. NP

OPPOSITE: A black swan nesting in raupo rushes. There are black swan populations at Hawksbury Lagoon, Blueskin Bay, Tomahawk, Hoopers and Papanui Inlets, Kaikorai Estuary and Lake Waihola.

George Chance

RIGHT: The shore crab *Hemigrapsus edwardsii* is common on sheltered shores in the mid-tide zone and is especially abundant in Otago Harbour. When threatened it will rock back on its hind legs and wave its claws menacingly. Its square back is purple and cream and can measure 50mm across. By day it hides under rocks when the tide is out and like many crabs scavenges for food. Octopuses and fish prey on it. NP

ESTUARY INSECTS

Saltmarsh insect life is surprisingly diverse, considering the relatively small extent of the habitat. Aramoana has over 80 moth species.

A high percentage of insects are diurnal. Many of the moths are day-flying, notably *Eutorna symmorpha*, whose larvae mine selliera leaves, and *Arctesthes catapyrrha*, whose larvae are found on plantago here.

Saltmarsh ribbonwood is the exclusive host of a small moth *Stigmella aigialeia*. One leaf will feed its leaf-mining caterpillar for a lifetime. At the other end of the scale is a geometrid moth *Pseudocoremia lactiflua*, whose looper larvae are capable of devouring tens of ribbonwood leaves.

ABOVE: A surprising find on saltmarsh on the west side of Rabbit Island in 1989 was the day-flying moth *Eurythecta leucothrinca*, whose recognised habitat is grassland in upland areas of Otago. The female of the species is flightless. It is thought to occur at sea level because the rocks of the Dunedin volcano depressed the eastern edge of the old Otago peneplain to sea level and below. BP

PENINSULA INLETS | A GODWIT HAVEN

Hoopers and Papanui Inlets on the ocean side of Otago Peninsula are bountiful for birds.

At Papanui (350ha), 44 species have been recorded, 24 of them regular users. Among the more unusual visitors is the glossy ibis, which wanders to New Zealand from Australia but has not begun breeding here yet. It belongs to the same family as royal spoonbill. Besides a regular array of seabirds, Papanui and Hoopers Inlets attract Australasian harrier (kāhu), New Zealand kingfisher (kōtare), paradise shelduck (pūtakitaki) and spur-winged plover.

A regular user in late spring and summer is the eastern bar-tailed godwit or kuaka *Limosa lapponica baueri*, which migrates to Australasia from breeding grounds in Siberia and northern Alaska. Flocks of 2000 godwits are not uncommon on the peninsula inlets at low tide, busily probing the mud and sand with their long, slightly upturned bills. Godwits often search for molluscs, crustaceans and worms in the company of South Island pied oystercatchers (tōrea), but are easily

ABOVE: Playgrounds for the tide: Hoopers and Papanui Inlets, viewed from the slopes of Sandymount. NP

RIGHT: A white-faced heron fishing in the shallows of Hoopers Inlet. NP

RIGHT: A pied stilt close to its nest site at Hoopers Inlet, Otago Peninsula. NP

distinguished from the black-and-white oystercatchers by their mottled brown plumage.

Among shellfish populations, cockles and pipi are abundant. Both inlets also have communities of crabs, notably the stalk-eyed mud crab, and burrowing anemones, and both are important nurseries for sand and green-back flounders.

Periodically, the entrance of Hoopers Inlet (380ha) is blocked with sand, and inlet water can submerge low-lying sections of road. In 1993, tidal access was blocked for months after a large landslip occurred at the former Sandymount Wildlife Refuge adjacent to the entrance. From 2011 to 2013, the Hoopers Inlet entrance was blocked again by sand and the inlet had reduced tidal effect, with periodic flooding of neighbouring roads during high tides and storm surges. The entrance was reopened in 2013 and the tidal cycle restored.

The saltmarsh around both inlets has been largely modified by roading or farmland development. At Hoopers Inlet, patches of copper tussock *Chionochloa rubra cuprea* grow behind surviving saltmarsh – a feature not found at Aramoana. At Papanui, peat outcrops on the southern fringe indicate that silver beech forest grew here between glaciations over 20,000 years ago.

Studies of the animal life in the saltmarsh and salt meadow of Hoopers Inlet have demonstrated the immense productivity of such habitats. At its maximum the microfauna (including amphipods, copepods, tardigrades, rotifers and nematodes) number 7.5 million animals per square metre.

OROKONUI INLET | A FISHY STORY

Orokonui Inlet, which feeds into the much larger Blueskin Bay Inlet, and its freshwater source, Orokonui Stream, are remarkable for their native fish populations. No fewer than 10 species have been recorded here – four galaxiids, three bullies, two eels and a lamprey.

Consequently, the area is prime habitat for New Zealand kingfishers. A tree planting programme along the banks of the stream, undertaken by school children as a conservation project, has enhanced the habitat.

Upstream, an old plantation of eucalypts features a tree that has become a tourist attraction because of its designation as New Zealand's tallest – a mountain ash *Eucalyptus regnans* which measured 81.26m in December 2013. It is accessible from Orokonui Ecosanctuary on Blueskin Road. A wild population of eastern rosellas, birds introduced from Australia, seems right at home here.

The Orokonui Inlet saltmarsh has prominent stands of jointed wire rush *Apodasmia similis* in association with the sedges *Isolepis marginata* and three-square *Schoenoplectus pungens*, and expanses of bachelor's button *Cotula coronopifolia*.

Near Waitati in Blueskin Bay there is a good example of saltmarsh grading into coastal shrubland remnants containing *Coprosma* species, ngaio, mānuka and Hall's tōtara. Across the inlet at Rabbit Island there is an excellent sequence of marsh grading into saltmarsh ribbonwood, New Zealand flax and silver tussock.

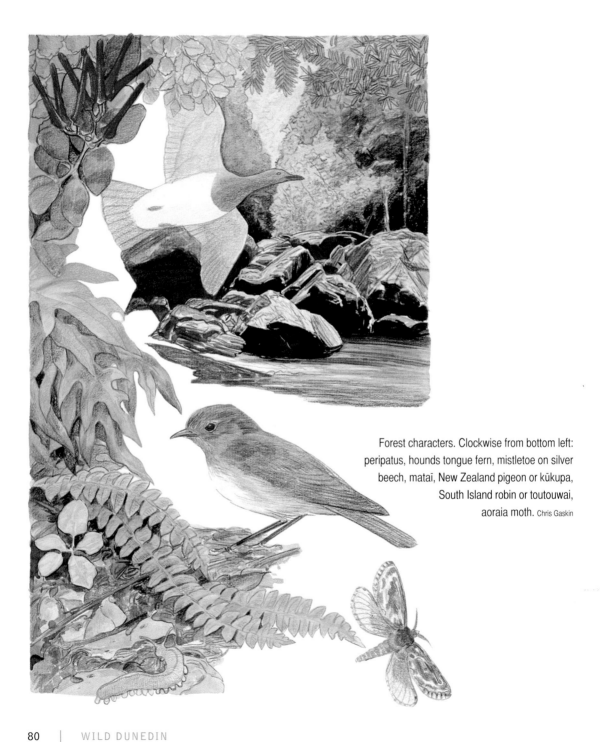

Forest characters. Clockwise from bottom left: peripatus, hounds tongue fern, mistletoe on silver beech, mataī, New Zealand pigeon or kūkupa, South Island robin or toutouwai, aoraia moth. Chris Gaskin

CHAPTER 6

FORESTS

TALL SURVIVORS

ABOVE: South Island robin *Petroica australis*, introduced to Orokonui Ecosanctuary from the Silver Peaks area, are well established in the Orokonui Valley forest. Their breeding success in the absence of predators has been extraordinary. They are often encountered by visitors using the ecosanctuary's valley track.

Dave Curtis

TWO HUNDRED years ago coastal Dunedin was a forested land of plenty. Dense forest and shrubland covered the land from sea level to the subalpine zone. Trees overhung harbour waters. Kākā filled the canopy with their melodious parrot calls. Mōhua (yellowhead) added canary colour and charming song. Brown kiwi were recorded calling as late as 1873, although there is some doubt about this record.

The bulk of the original forest cover disappeared in the latter half of the nineteenth century following the arrival of European settlers, who felled the impressive podocarps, mainly rimu, miro, kahikatea, mataī and tōtara, for building timber. Lowland forest occupied land that was required for farming, so it had to go. The least promising patches survived. They included higher forest and the more remote stands. Today, they combine with regenerating shrubland to give the city – the hilly eastern parts anyway – a reasonably leafy countenance. Plantation forests of *Pinus radiata* and Douglas fir have been imposed on the landscape – geometric and uniformly dark green.

Around metropolitan Dunedin the forest would have been dominated by tall podocarp trees. In the sub-canopy we can picture such medium-sized trees as lemonwood or tarata *Pittosporum eugenioides*, scenting the air in spring with profuse yellow blooms, marbleleaf or putaputaweta *Carpodetus serratus*, broadleaf *Griselinia littoralis*, whiteywood or māhoe *Melicytus ramiflorus* and the world's largest tree fuchsia, kōtukutuku *Fuchsia excorticata*, whose delicious, dark purple drupes ripen in early summer for birds to gorge upon. These species are still common and regenerate well. The Leith Valley, notably Nicols Creek, holds some outstanding specimens of kōtukutuku.

At higher sites, and especially inland, the tall forest is more likely to comprise silver beech *Lophozonia menziesii*, often in association with the podocarps tōtara and mataī. The Waipori Valley is a silver beech stronghold. Small patches occur on the slopes of Mt Cargill, Flagstaff and Mihiwaka facing Otago Harbour – the closest silver beech to metropolitan Dunedin. There are larger stands on the slopes of Maungātua and the Silver Peaks and at Evansdale, usually with Hall's tōtara, and a few trees are spread among the podocarps in the Taieri River forest close to sea level near Taieri Mouth.

Fossil pollen studies suggest that 6000–8000 years ago, when there was a milder climate with less seasonal difference, tōtara and mataī forest was much more extensive on inland sites now occupied by silver beech. A climate change – towards seasonal extremes of cold, wet winters and warm, dry summers – favoured the spread of silver beech. Natural fires and those caused by early Māori made inroads on the forest to the benefit of the fire-tolerant tussock grasslands.

ABOVE: Orokonui Ecosanctuary head guide, Sue Hensley, is greeted by a friendly resident kākā called Mr Roto at the start of an after-dark tour. NP

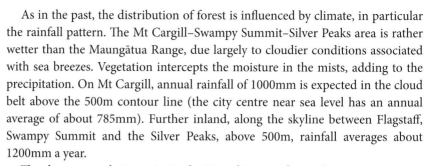

As in the past, the distribution of forest is influenced by climate, in particular the rainfall pattern. The Mt Cargill–Swampy Summit–Silver Peaks area is rather wetter than the Maungātua Range, due largely to cloudier conditions associated with sea breezes. Vegetation intercepts the moisture in the mists, adding to the precipitation. On Mt Cargill, annual rainfall of 1000mm is expected in the cloud belt above the 500m contour line (the city centre near sea level has an annual average of about 785mm). Further inland, along the skyline between Flagstaff, Swampy Summit and the Silver Peaks, above 500m, rainfall averages about 1200mm a year.

The absence or relative rarity in the Dunedin area of several native tree species has long puzzled botanists. Southern rātā *Metrosideros umbellata*, so common in the South Otago coastal forest, runs out just south of Taieri Mouth. Kāmahi *Weinmannia racemosa*, common in the south and on the West Coast, also meets a natural boundary at Taieri Mouth. The only naturally occurring kāmahi in Dunedin are a few specimens in Mill Creek (southern Maungātua) and the Leith Valley, and at Grahams Bush between Sawyers Bay and Mt Cargill.

Compared to northern regions, the Dunedin forest contains only a small number of tall tree species. But the sub-canopy and understorey trees, shrubs and lianes are a diverse lot, adding delightful variation in form and colour.

OROKONUI ECOSANCTUARY | A HAVEN FOR RARE WILDLIFE

A new concept in nature conservation – a predator-fenced sanctuary – was opened to the public on the outskirts of Dunedin in October 2009. Orokonui Ecosanctuary, the first project of its kind in the South Island, has become the biodiversity and conservation flagship for the Otago region.

Spanning 307ha of the Orokonui Valley near Waitati, the ecosanctuary is creating a healthy indigenous ecosystem free of introduced mammalian predators. An 8.7km predator-exclusion fence surrounds a mixed kānuka and podocarp forest, with extensive patches of regenerating broadleaf forest, a stand of eucalyptus trees at the bottom end of the valley (including New Zealand's tallest tree, an 81m mountain ash) and grassy open areas near the top.

After the fence was completed in 2007, an intensive pest eradication programme was carried out to rid the area of possums, goats, hares, hedgehogs, rabbits, ferrets, stoats, weasels, cats, rats and mice. Meanwhile, the Otago Natural History Trust, which established the project at a cost of about $5.5 million, made plans for the reintroduction of species lost to the valley through predators and land modification.

By the end of 2013, South Island kākā, South Island saddleback, South Island robin, Haast tokoeka (the rarest of the kiwi), jewelled gecko, green skink, takahē, tuatara, longfin eels and Otago skinks had been released into the ecosanctuary. The Otago skinks were released into a subenclosure enriched with schist rock slabs, their favoured habitat. The uncommon South Island fernbird (mātātā) has established itself within the fenced area, encouraged by the haven qualities. The

ABOVE: Holding a young Haast tokoeka before its release at Orokonui Ecosanctuary in December 2012 is Dr Jean Fleming of Otago University. Kiwi have begun calling in the wild in Dunedin for the first time in over 130 years.

Matt Thomson

ABOVE: Eight-year-old Mihai Whitaker, of Waitati, releases a juvenile tuatara into its burrow at Orokonui Ecosanctuary in 2012 under the guidance of Conservation Manager Elton Smith. NP

translocated rare species have joined about a dozen species of native birds already established there, including rifleman (tītīpounamu), the smallest of the New Zealand birds, and flocking brown creepers.

Although the flighted species are free to fly over the fence, the highly mobile kākā began breeding within the ecosanctuary soon after their release and by 2013 the population at Orokonui had reached 30. Following a second translocation of robins, this species too is now well settled at the ecosanctuary.

Rare or uncommon plant species have also been reintroduced to help round out the ecosystem restoration. Since the removal of predators inside the fence, there has been spectacular regeneration of shrubs and trees such as five-finger, tree fuchsia and wineberry, which were formerly targeted by possums and goats. Birdsong has returned to the valley, led by the bellbirds and tūī almost always seen at the feeding stations scattered around the reserve.

The network of tracks inside the fence caters for all ages and abilities, and includes a track that extends more than 2km to near the bottom of the valley. An extensive visitor centre is located at the top of the ecosanctuary, off Blueskin Road. The sustainably designed building offers striking views across the valley to the upper Silver Stream catchment and the Silver Peaks. Inside is an array of information panels, a café, a shop and an education centre that caters for school visits. Orokonui Ecosanctuary is a powerful advocate for nature conservation. Visitors not only enjoy recreation in the ecosanctuary but also gain new knowledge of, and commitment to, conservation.

ABOVE: Kiwi footprints in the snow at Orokonui Ecosanctuary. Alyth Grant

KAPUKATAUMAHAKA | MT CARGILL'S OTHER NAME

The highest peak overlooking Otago Harbour is named after Captain William Cargill, co-founder of Otago's Scottish settlement (1848). But Mt Cargill (680m) has another name – Kapukataumahaka. Within this single Māori word is a tale that combines botany, birdlife and bush survival skills.

Kāpuka is the name for broadleaf *Griselinia littoralis*, and taumahaka refers to the snaring of birds at a water trough. The slopes of Mt Cargill were renowned for their kāpuka trees, which attracted kūkupa, the New Zealand pigeon (also known as kererū or kūkū). When the pigeons ate kāpuka berries they became thirsty, hence the use of water troughs by Māori hunters, who set snares over them.

Broadleaf is abundant today around Dunedin in sub-canopy situations and in open or disturbed areas, reaching a height of about 15m. It is among the hardiest of New Zealand's trees, growing up to 900m above sea level and capable of enduring very dry conditions. Its flowers are greenish and so, too, are the immature fruits, which darken when ready to drop.

LEITH SADDLE | PODOCARP POTPOURRI

An outstanding podocarp-cedar forest greets travellers at the high point on Dunedin's northern motorway – Leith Saddle, 390m above sea level. In addition to the dark green conical form of New Zealand cedar or kaikawaka *Libocedrus bidwillii*, the emergent trees are chiefly of the podocarp group – rimu *Dacrydium cupressinum*, miro *Prumnopitys ferruginea* (both near their upper limit) and Hall's or thin-barked tōtara *Podocarpus cunninghamii*.

Rimu, recognisable by its drooping olive-green foliage, and tōtara both produce seed that rests neatly on a small, brightly coloured basal fruit (hence the name podocarp – 'seed on a foot'); miro, belonging to a genus that means 'plum fruit', produces drupes that contain the seed. The drupe is large, reddish and irresistible to New Zealand pigeons.

Medium-sized trees of māhoe, kōtukutuku and three-finger (orihou) *Pseudopanax colensoi* overtop shrubs that include the abundant hūpiro *Coprosma foetidissima*, whose crushed leaves smell of dung, hence its unflattering common name stinkwood. In the New Zealand forest there is nothing quite like kōtukutuku *Fuchsia excorticata* and from the Leith Saddle boardwalk it can be inspected close up. The bark is orange-brown, tissue thin and always peeling; the flowers are a mixture of green, red and purple and the pollen a vivid blue – colours that speak of this tree's tropical origins.

Notable ground-cover plants are the crown fern *Blechnum discolor* and the bush lily *Astelia fragrans*. Among the abundant epiphytic filmy ferns hang the curiously shaped stems of *Tmesipteris tannensis*, the most primitive of vascular plants, with curved pointed leaf-like blades.

LEITH VALLEY | RAINFOREST AND GLOW WORMS

On the city side of the Leith Saddle, the valley features rainforest that has an abundance and diversity of bryophytes to rival Fiordland. Nicols Falls is a 12m-high forest-enclosed waterfall on a tributary of the Leith. It takes 15 minutes on foot from the Leith Valley Road and at one time was a popular scenic attraction for visitors and Dunedin residents, complemented after dark by a display of glow worms on the ravine walls of Nicols Creek. The glow worm *Arachnocampa luminosa* is the larva of a native fly (a long-legged fungus gnat, seldom seen). To catch food, the 2–4cm-long larvae lower sticky threads and attract prey by

FAR LEFT: Kōtukutuku tree fuchsia overtops a garden of the bush lily *Astelia fragrans* on the Leith Saddle track. Some leaves of the astelia have been eaten by caterpillars. NP

CENTRE: Conical New Zealand cedars (kaikawaka) are a feature of the Leith Saddle forest canopy. NP

ABOVE: Mānuka flowering profusely in shrubland above the Leith Saddle forest. NP

ABOVE: New Zealand pigeon or kūkupa *Hemiphaga novaeseelandiae* is one of the most conspicuous birds of the Leith Valley–Woodhaugh–Botanic Gardens area. Kōwhai flowers and miro fruit figure prominently in the diet of these birds, which play a key role in forest ecology as seed dispersers. They are among the world's most beautifully coloured pigeon species. They nest in trees and raise a single chick each breeding season. When laden with miro berries, kūkupa fly sluggishly with a characteristic whistling laboured wingbeat. But they can be surprisingly agile in the air. In what is thought to be territorial displays, they will perform a highly spectacular pattern of stalls and swoops. NP

RIGHT: Lifecycle of the glow worm: Hatching from the egg (centre top) the worm-like larva builds a 'hammock' from which it hangs and illuminates sticky threads that fish for prey. The lights can be turned on and off, and the worm slides back and forth in its 'hammock'. A pupa is the next stage, from which the gnat appears. Chris Gaskin emitting a bluish light that can be turned off and on at will. The New Zealand glow worm, which has a 12-month life cycle, is not related to its European namesake, which is a beetle that uses light to attract a mate.

WOODHAUGH | RELICT SWAMP FOREST

Within Woodhaugh Gardens on the banks of the Water of Leith lies a small remnant of kahikatea swamp forest – the only example left in Dunedin district. Kahikatea or white pine *Dacrycarpus dacrydioides* was once abundant in fertile low-lying areas, typically on alluvial soils. New Zealand's tallest native tree, reaching 60m, it was plundered last century for its soft, pale and odourless timber, valuable for old-style butter boxes. A few specimens are prominent with mataī in pasture on the river flats near Waitati, close to State Highway 1, and there are a number of large kahikatea trees on the banks of the Taieri River upstream from the Taieri Mouth bridge and at Woodside on the Taieri Plain.

At Woodhaugh the kahikatea is associated with mataī or black pine, lacebark and lowland ribbonwood. Some of the native trees in the vicinity have been planted, notably red beech *Fuscopora fusca*.

Prominent sub-canopy trees are tarata *Pittosporum eugenioides*, māhoe *Melicytus ramiflorus* and milk tree or tūrepo *Streblus heterophyllus*, whose common name refers to the milky sap that exudes from the stems in spring. Less common at Woodhaugh and in the Dunedin area generally is a shrubby small-leaved relative of māhoe, *Melicytus micranthus*. Found perching on a variety of shrubs and trees is the broad-leaved mistletoe *Ileostylus micranthus*, which has tiny yellow flowers and yellow berries.

ABOVE: October blossoms in the Leith Valley / Pine Hill area – lemonwood or tarata *Pittosporum eugenioides* flowers prolifically in spring. Its common name derives from the lemon scent exuded by the leaves when crushed. Lemonwood resin was used by Māori as chewing gum. NP

LEFT: Silvereye feeding on nectar of kōwhai *Sophora microphylla* in full flower on the cliffs above Woodhaugh Gardens. The flowers attract numerous birds, including tūī, bellbird, and New Zealand pigeon. At least five moth species specialise in feeding on various parts of the kōwhai. NP

ABOVE, LEFT: Southern rātā flowering in the Town Belt. Rātā does not grow naturally in the city. NP

ABOVE, RIGHT: Marbleleaf or putaputaweta *Carpodetus serratus* produces abundant flowers in December–January. An attractive New Zealand endemic, it grows to about 10m. It is host to a parasitic shrub, the mistletoe *Tupeia antarctica* (tāpia or pirita), whose white, purple-flecked berries were a food of the Māori. Besides marbleleaf, host plants for this mistletoe include species of coprosma, pittosporum, pseudopanax and hoheria. In the Dunedin area it has been recorded in the Town Belt and Woodhaugh Gardens, and at Kuri Bush near Taieri Mouth. NP

TOWN BELT

A 4.5km-long green belt dissects the hill suburbs of metropolitan Dunedin between the Southern Cemetery and the Botanic Gardens, providing the city with a conspicuous array of native and introduced trees dating from the nineteenth century. Following the clearance of much of the area, native and introduced species were planted in many areas and regeneration filled out the protected corridor known as the Town Belt. More than 200 tree and shrub species are found here.

At the northern end, the light-demanding kānuka *Kunzea ericoides* is a feature tree, occupying drier sites. Its presence indicates total clearance of the original forest cover. Some kānuka – 30cm in diameter and 15m tall – are overmature and beginning to collapse. Associated with kānuka are broadleaf *Griselinia littoralis*, māpou *Myrsine australis* and patē *Schefflera digitata*. Another prominent tree is kōtukutuku *Fuchsia excorticata*, which relishes the shady faces found across much of the Town Belt.

Remnant tall podocarps are dotted throughout and there are a few young self-sown rimu, tōtara and mataī establishing. Lacebark *Hoheria populnea* (naturalised here from the North Island) and its narrow-leaved cousin *H. angustifolia* are represented, as is lowland ribbonwood or manatū *Plagianthus regius*, a tree reaching 17m with form and foliage vastly different from saltmarsh ribbonwood. There are large planted specimens of red beech *Fuscopora fusca*

PROBLEM PLANTS

Old man's beard *Clematis vitalba*, a noxious deciduous climber, delights in establishing in areas such as the Town Belt. Without control, it will invade and eventually overwhelm native vegetation.

It was introduced into New Zealand last century as an ornamental plant but has since spread to become a threat in many areas. It is well-known for its grey tufted seed balls that are conspicuous in autumn and persist through winter after the leaves are lost. Older stems are grey and ribbed; younger stems are purple and downy.

Old man's beard is difficult to control. It must be dug out by the roots to be destroyed. Broken bits left lying around will readily resprout. The cut roots or stumps can be poisoned and the foliage burnt. Other problem plants include bomarea, banana passionfruit, Darwin's barberry and Chilean flame creeper.

and southern rātā *Metrosideros umbellata*. Several shrubs outside their natural limits also thrive in the Town Belt, notably rangiora *Brachyglottis repanda* and raurēkau *Coprosma grandiflora*. Rangiora, which bears unmistakably large oblong leaves, white underneath, forms hedges if trimmed, as on the road to Purakaunui above Port Chalmers. Its natural southern limit is Kaikoura.

Throughout the Town Belt, and colouring it in autumn, are magnificent examples of exotic deciduous trees, now fully mature, including European beech, English oak, sycamore and elm. Towards the southern end especially, they create a woodland effect.

The leaf litter fauna, as in forest environments throughout New Zealand, is rich in spiders, insects and micro-snails. One tiny snail from the Town Belt, *Alsolemia cresswelli*, is a Dunedin endemic species. A recent survey recorded 46 micro-snail species in the metropolitan area.

CAVERSHAM | PERIPATUS

In the leaf litter of Caversham Valley's moist bushed gullies, which form the southern limit of the Town Belt, lives a small velvety caterpillar-like creature of exceptional interest to science. Growing to over 3cm in length, it belongs to an ancient group of invertebrates called peripatus (ngaokeoke) – believed to be the missing link between worms (annelida) and the centipedes, insects, spiders and crustaceans (arthropoda).

Although resembling a caterpillar or centipede, the peripatus does not have a head marked off from the rest of the body nor any external sign of segmentation. Only about a hundred species of peripatus are known to science, although it is a group spread across Southeast Asia, Africa, South America, Australia and New Zealand. While some species lay eggs, others give birth to live young and some even have a placenta through which nutrients are delivered to developing embryos.

Young of the Caversham peripatus are born alive and family groups stay together for some time. The Caversham animal is a voracious carnivore. To entrap its prey it shoots out streams of sticky

TUNNELWEB SPIDER

Among the more distinctive spiders of the Dunedin forest is the large, colourful and common tunnelweb spider *Porrhothele antipodiana,* which builds thick webs under logs and stones. The first New Zealand spider to be named, it is popularly known as the Andersons Bay spider because many of its kind are found there.

The tunnelweb spider possesses many primitive features such as the up-and-down movements of its fangs and the presence of four book lungs on the underside of its abdomen. This method of breathing means it must seek out dark and moist habitats where prey consists of beetles and other invertebrates.

Despite its somewhat awesome appearance it is not poisonous, but it may bite if squeezed or handled roughly. The male tunnelweb spider wanders about during the mating season and at this time may enter buildings. The best way to deal with them is to coax them gently into a jar and deposit them outside. BP

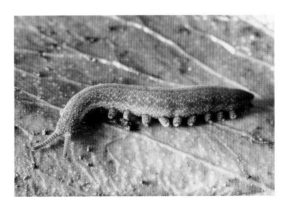

ABOVE: The Caversham peripatus. BP

ABOVE: New Zealand long-tailed bat *Chalinolobus tuberculatus*, one of the world's micro-bats, has been reported from the Silver Stream forest. The nearest populations are in the Catlins. Rod Morris

fluid from turrets on either side of its head. Despite urban development and the clearance of much of its habitat, this peripatus has survived. Both the Caversham species and a new species from the Leith Valley are of international significance. Peripatus are also found at Orokonui Ecosanctuary. In 1993 the Dunedin City Council, with the assistance of the Royal Forest and Bird Protection Society, purchased a 4ha area of Caversham Bush to extend and protect the habitat of this extraordinary animal. Its conservation status was an issue during the 2011–13 Caversham Valley motorway-widening project but its habitat was extended in a land swap and remained protected.

SILVER STREAM | REFUGE FOR ROBINS

Small populations of South Island robin or toutouwai *Petroica australis* inhabit native and planted forests in the Silver Stream catchment in the vicinity of Whare Flat as well as in Douglas fir plantations in the Silver Peaks area and at Orokonui Ecosanctuary. As the only robins in east Otago, these populations are of major interest to ornithologists and conservationists. Robins require forested areas to disperse and are unlikely ever to have contact with the nearest populations – on the Blue Mountains and at Waikaia Bush in northern Southland, 115km west. The Silver Stream robins' habitat includes kānuka, mānuka and regenerating native broad-leaved forest, but the birds were also found in old plantations of exotic trees in the Flagstaff block until the plantations were logged. Commonly encountered on or close to the forest floor (hence their vulnerability to stoats, wild cats and other predators), they eat insects and other invertebrates and will draw near to people strolling in their territories in the hope the intruders will inadvertently stir up new food. Orokonui Ecosanctuary's population had grown from 17 in 2010 to 235 by 2014 thanks to the predator exclusion fence.

WAIPORI | SILVER BEECH STRONGHOLD

Waipori Valley, south of Maungātua, contains the largest remnant silver beech forest in the eastern South Island north of the Catlins region. Silver beech is spread throughout Waipori Falls Scenic Reserve (1322ha), Dunedin's largest scenic reserve, which occupies the central portion of the valley. Across about a quarter of the reserve it forms a pure forest; elsewhere it is emergent with podocarp trees, mainly rimu, matāi, and tōtara, or gives way to kānuka/mānuka woodland. From the mouth of the gorge it expands across the southern face of Maungātua and is clearly visible from the Taieri Plain.

Silver beech or tawhai is the most widely distributed of New Zealand's five kinds of beech (red, hard, silver, mountain and black). It forms the treeline through much of the wetter regions of western Otago and Fiordland. None of the other beech species – the larger-leaved red and hard beech and the smaller-leaved, smooth-edged mountain and black beech – is found naturally in the Dunedin area, although there are planted examples of them all, especially red beech.

The Waipori forest is bordered in the south by an extensive planted forest of *Pinus radiata* and in the north by shrubland and tussock grassland on the shoulder of the Maungātua Range. The native forest is a mosaic of types. A visitor

ABOVE: Silver beech forest flanking Waipori River. NP

LEFT: A pair of South Island riflemen *Acanthisitta chloris* at their nest, with food for chicks. The rifleman is New Zealand's smallest native bird. Another small forest bird, restricted to South Island forests, is brown creeper or pīpipi *Mohoua novaeseelandiae*. It is common in Waipori forest and at Orokonui Ecosanctuary. In the non-breeding season flocks of brown creepers trickle through the canopy, keeping contact with a repetitive trilling call and often in the company of numbers of silvereyes, grey warblers and South Island fantails. Brown creeper is a host for the migratory long-tailed cuckoo. Rod Morris

BELOW: Prickly shield fern *Polystichum vestitum*, Waipori Valley. NP

RIGHT: Mistletoe *Perixilla colensi* in Waipori beech forest. NP

can sample beech, podocarp, kānuka and a range of broad-leaved trees on the walking tracks in the vicinity of the picnic ground in the lower valley. The same area hosts an array of birdlife, including bellbird (kōmako/makomako), grey warbler (kōriroriro/riroriro), silvereye (tauhou), brown creeper (pīpipi), South Island fantail (pīwakawaka), New Zealand pigeon (kūkupa/kererū) and shining cuckoo (pīpīwharauroa).

The silver beech trees are host to red mistletoe *Peraxilla colensoi* (pikiraki), which produces abundant scarlet flowers in December–January. There is a good place to see mistletoe halfway up the valley at a clearing on the banks of the Waipori River. Another accessible red mistletoe habitat is close to the picnic ground at Woodside, upstream of which large silver beech trees are garlanded with flowers of the parasite at the festive season.

The Waipori forest is home to a rich assortment of insects, among them the only Dunedin records of the moths *Austrocidaria parora* and *Asaphodes obarata*, the latter nationally rare.

EASTERN ROSELLA

Larger and much more brightly coloured than native parakeets, eastern rosellas have established wild populations on the outskirts of the Dunedin metropolitan area since their introduction from Australia in about 1910. Singly or in flocks, they are reasonably common in the upper Leith Valley (especially around Sullivans Dam), Waitati and Orokonui Ecosanctuary, Woodside (west Taieri) and Waipori Valley. They favour forest margins and lightly wooded areas, and nest in spring, mainly in holes in trees. Their call when alarmed is a loud parrot-like screech.

FOREST MOTHS

The zigzag moth *Charixena iridoxa* (TOP), whose white larvae live in the base of astelia leaves. Although the larvae remain more or less stationary, their feeding produces a zigzag effect on the leaves emerging from the base. Mt Cargill and the cliffs below Cargill's Castle near St Clair have the only colonies of this moth in Dunedin City. It is mainly found in the mountains of the Main Divide.

Another moth *Tmetolophota purdii*, more widespread, feeds on astelia. Its fat green caterpillars create large holes on the leaves (see page 85). The handsome orange adult was first described from Fairfield. BP

Featured on the $100 note, the zebra moth *Declana egregia* (RIGHT) is common in the higher-altitude forests of Dunedin where the cryptic larvae feed on three-finger foliage. The adults are nocturnal and depend on their resemblance to tree-trunk lichens for camouflage by day. BP

The elegant moth *Hydriomena arida* was first described from Dunedin and thought to be locally extinct until it was rediscovered in damp gullies in the Leith Valley. A nocturnal moth, the larvae feed on *Gunnera monoica* on damp banks. BP

The exquisitely coloured moth *Phycomorpha metachrysa* is the smaller of two uncommon moths whose larvae are found feeding on milk tree *Streblus heterophyllus* in Woodhaugh Gardens. The larger of the two is *Meterana octans* (RIGHT), whose fat bright-green larvae are well camouflaged in the foliage of the milk tree. The former was first described from the Dunedin area, and its larvae feed within the diseased spikes of the plant. BP

Dunedin is the only New Zealand city with a resident species of aoraia, a large ghost moth. Adult males of *Aoraia rufivena*, (BOTTOM) which have a wingspan of about 7cm, are often attracted to city lights. The winged but flightless female scatters eggs about the forest floor. The species also occurs in snowgrass communities. It has an annual lifecycle, with adults emerging between late January and May. Despite its size and conspicuousness, this moth was named only recently, in 1994. It is related to the native porina moths which are pests of exotic pasture. BP

Uplands symbols.
Clockwise from bottom left:
Lycopodium club moss, *Blechnum novae-zelandiae* or kiokio fern, three-finger shrub or orihou, tussock butterfly *Argyrophenga janitae*, New Zealand cedar or kaikawaka, South Island tomtit or ngirungiru, peppertree or horopito.

Chris Gaskin

CHAPTER **7** | # UPLANDS

HIGH COUNTRY POTPOURRI

BEYOND the coastal hills and the angular volcanic peaks overlooking Otago Harbour is a largely treeless upland environment of exposed ridges and plateaux, snow tussock communities, shrubby gullies and wetlands. Not as high as the ranges on the city perimeter (Maungātua, Lammermoor and Rock and Pillar) but skyline-makers nonetheless, the uplands include landscape features such as the Silver Peaks (777m), Swampy Summit (739m) and neighbouring Flagstaff (668m), Swampy Hill (733m) on the northern boundary of the city near Nenthorn, Mt Watkin (616m) inland from Waikouaiti, and Taieri Ridge (708m).

The Swampy–Flagstaff complex separates the Leith and Silver Stream catchments; the Silver Peaks main ridge divides the Waikouaiti and Taieri catchments; Mt Watkin holds the high ground to the north of the Waikouaiti River's north branch; and Taieri Ridge separates the Strath Taieri from the Moonlight–Macraes district.

Except for Flagstaff, which lies on a popular walking track overlooking the city centre, these upland features are little visited; but they are well worth exploring for their distinctive array of plants and fauna. Among the most surprising aspects is the presence of extensive and species-rich wetlands, a habitat more commonly associated with valley floors.

Before Mt Cargill Road and the more modern northern motorway were built, the main route north to Waikouaiti lay across the open country and moderate grades of Flagstaff and Swampy Summit, which were called the Snowy Mountains for a time. Known to Māori as Whakāri (after which the adjacent suburb of Wakari is named) Flagstaff is like a forehead on the city landscape, high and prominent. It acquired its European name from the nineteenth-century practice of hoisting a flag at its high point to let European settlers on the Taieri know of the arrival of an immigrant vessel at Port Chalmers or Dunedin.

Flagstaff and Swampy Summit are volcanic creations, as is the solitary round knob of Mt Watkin. The Silver Peaks and Taieri Ridge are built of schist, although there are volcanic protuberances on Taieri Ridge in the form of The Sisters and The Crater.

The land tenure of the uplands is mixed. The designations include scenic reserve (Department of Conservation and Dunedin City Council), water and timber reserve (City Council), pastoral leasehold and freehold. About 2500ha of land in the Silver Peaks area formerly managed by the City Council as water and timber reserve are now included in the Silver Peaks Scenic Reserve, making this reserve one of Otago's largest at over 3500ha.

KAIKAWAKA

The pyramidal or cone form of New Zealand cedar or kaikawaka *Libocedrus bidwillii* stands out in the cloud forest of Leith Saddle. It also cuts a striking profile in high forest in the Silver Peaks area and on the flanks of Mt Cargill, Flagstaff and Swampy Summit.

After about 15 minutes' climb up the Leith Saddle Track, one is rewarded by a close encounter with a rich native cedar forest. Kaikawaka grows to a height of about 15m on this ridge. The trunk is tapered, the bark light brown and decidedly stringy. Lower branches are bulky and often jut at right angles to the trunk, making the tree's distinctive form.

Old spars, silvery with age and clearly hard-wearing, are prominently scattered about the canopy. The death of so many cedars while still standing may be due to climate change.

KĀHU | AUSTRALASIAN HARRIER

A feature of upland areas is the Australasian harrier or kāhu *Circus approximans*, pictured here feeding on a dead hare. A large bird of prey, it is typically seen gliding across open areas with its long wings forming a shallow V. Harriers nest around swamps over summer, following a courtship that usually involves spectacular diving, soaring and tumbling flights. About the only time their calls are heard is at courtship – a high-pitched plaintive 'see-oo'.

Since European settlement, harriers have increased in number and extended their range due to the clearance of forest and the introduction of small mammals, notably rabbits, which have served to increase their food supply. Although they will take live prey, they readily scavenge road kills and are themselves often run down by vehicles.

The harrier, self-introduced from Australia, is about a third larger than the endemic New Zealand falcon (see page 113), our only other surviving daytime bird of prey.
ROD MORRIS

ABOVE: The horizontal orchid *Waireia stenopetala* on a moss bed, Swampy Summit. NP

UPLAND FLOWERS

Sun orchids of the genus *Thelymitra* are eye-catching on Swampy Summit and Flagstaff in late summer and early autumn. Sometimes found singly, sometimes in groups, the sun orchids present their flowers on tall stalks. Two species (*T. cyanea* and *T. hatchii*) have blue flowers; the more common *T. longifolia* has white ones with purple and yellow centres. Other ground orchids common in upland grasslands or near bush or forest are the white orchid *Stegostyla lyallii*; the horizontal or beak orchid *Waireia stenopetala*, which holds its yellow-green flowers (usually two) curiously horizontal; the odd-leaved orchid *Aporostylis bifolia*, which has two unequally sized hairy leaves and white flowers with yellow dots on the lip; and the onion orchid *Microtis unifolia*, which has only one leaf and arranges its myriad tiny yellow-green flowers on a tall spike.

Celmisia hookeri, an uncommon native daisy, is found on the sweeping upland plateau of Swampy Hill 25km northwest of Waikouaiti near Dunedin's northern boundary and in a rare plants garden at Orokonui Ecosanctuary. Its large, soft leaves form rosettes up to about 50cm wide. Its last refuges are in northeast Otago, including the Horse Range, and, somewhat surprisingly, northern Southland (Nokomai Gorge; Slate Range). The daisy has suffered from grazing, fires and unscrupulous collecting for garden use. A rare grass *Simplicia laxa* was recently rediscovered at Nenthorn near Swampy Hill.

SNOW TUSSOCKS

Tall snow tussocks give the uplands a distinctive tawny colour and soft texture. Where undisturbed, they develop impressive size and density, and will grow to over 2m in height – a low 'forest', long-lived.

The most important tussock species in the Dunedin uplands – and across the Otago rangelands – is narrow-leaved snow tussock *Chionochloa rigida*. Its flowerheads overtop the leaves, a habit which distinguishes it from red tussock *C. rubra*, whose flowerheads are generally held within the foliage. Red tussock's southern subspecies, *C. rubra cuprea*, known also as copper tussock on account of the colour of its leaves, mixes with narrow-leaved snow tussock on Swampy Summit. A larger but less abundant species, *C. conspicua*, more commonly associated with shrubland and forest margins, has broader leaves and conspicuous flowerheads that are similar to but more branched than toetoe *Cortaderia richardii*.

Over the last thousand years, fires lit by early Māori allowed tussock grassland to spread into areas once dominated by forest or shrubland.

Tussock is a word derived from the Old English term 'tusk', meaning a tuft of hair. Indeed, tall tussocks are hair-like on the landscape, waving and rippling in the wind.

ABOVE: A magnificent specimen of *Celmisia hookeri*, bearing flowers up to 70mm across, at Orokonui Ecosanctuary's Otago Rare Plants Garden. NP

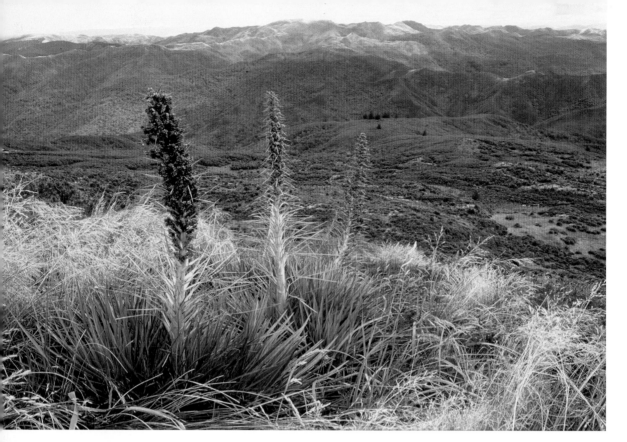

SWAMPY SUMMIT–FLAGSTAFF

'A wonderful gift of Nature to Dunedin.'
– A.H. Reed (publisher/writer), describing Flagstaff, 1954

For anyone interested in botany and insects, the adjoining tops of Swampy Summit and Flagstaff represent a fascinating subalpine experience within sight and easy striking distance of the city centre.

Speargrass is one of the most distinctive plants. Swampy Summit is a key habitat for *Aciphylla scott-thomsonii*, the tallest and stoutest of New Zealand's 40-odd species of speargrass (type locality, Maungātua Range). Its massive clumps of stiff glaucous (blue-green) leaves can reach over 1m in height, out of which rise flower heads up to 3m tall. Although common on Swampy Summit, it is scarce on neighbouring Flagstaff, where the smaller golden speargrass *A. aurea* prevails. The latter, common throughout the Otago uplands, has leaves edged in yellow. The whole plant has a golden hue. *A. glaucescens* is smaller, with narrow bluish-green leaves. The slender-leaved *A. subflabellata* is found on the northwest slopes of Swampy Summit, towards the Silver Peaks area. Its southern limit is Black Head but it may be extinct there. A small colony survives among flax on the cliffs south of St Clair.

The genus *Aciphylla* is found only in New Zealand and Australia, with Australia having just two species. Botanists have long puzzled over why they evolved such sharp armoury in a land that lacked browsing mammals. One theory held that the spines and needle-tipped leaves constituted a defence against trampling and

ABOVE: Tauhinu or cottonwood *Ozothamnus vauvilliersii* in flower, growing over a bed of the colourful fern kiokio *Blechnum novae-zelandiae* on Swampy Summit. NP

browsing by moa. But there is also speculation that the spines are not a defence at all but an evolutionary response to chronic drought in the distant past. Another benefit of the stiff spiny foliage is that it enables the plant to create room for itself among the snow tussocks and shrubs.

Across the Swampy Summit–Flagstaff tops the vegetation is dominated by snow tussock and mountain flax *Phormium cookianum*. Post-European fires induced a comprehensive cover of snow tussock but the shrubs are reinvading in many areas. Mānuka *Leptospermum scoparium*, inaka or grass tree *Dracophyllum longifolium* and tauhinu or cottonwood *Ozothamnus vauvilliersii* are migrating upwards from strongholds near the forest edge. Other shrubs making inroads on the tussock grasslands are *Hebe odora*, notable for its neatly rounded bushes and clusters of white flowers at the branch tips, three-finger *Pseudopanax colensoi*, which produces flowers (white) and fruit (purple-black) on large umbels, and the tree daisy *Olearia aborescens*. Mānuka is expected to predominate in the medium term, with the likelihood it will eventually be succeeded by native forest (New Zealand cedar/broadleaf), if fire can be excluded. Grasslands are expected to persist longer on the cooler tops, however. The shrubland / forest succession has prompted a suggestion that the lower slopes of the Flagstaff area be burnt every 15 to 20 years in spring, in order to retain the snow tussock cover for which the scenic reserve was created, as well as for its educational, ecological and recreational values.

There is a threat of wilding tree infestation from the large plantation of exotic trees (mainly *Pinus radiata*, Douglas fir and European larch) growing on the southwestern slopes of Flagstaff and Swampy Summit.

Wetter conditions on the top of Swampy Summit, where there are peat layers and extensive bogs, could inhibit the development of woody species much beyond what is already established – low-growing shrubs such as *Coprosma cheesemanii*, *C. ciliata* and *C. rugosa*, the daphne relative *Pimelea oreophila*, and an occasional turpentine shrub *Dracophyllum uniflorum*, which is a bronze-leaved, more prostrate relative of the Grass tree. Among the *Coprosma* species, *C. rugosa* stands out because of its reddish-brown bark. Swampy Summit has two species of the poisonous shrub tutu – the broad-leaved *Coriaria sarmentosa* and feathery-leaved *C. plumosa*.

Dwarf shrubs filling gaps between tussocks and flax, and often only ankle-high, include *Pentachondra pumila*, which is distinguished by its relatively large scarlet berries (up to 12mm diameter and hollow), *Androstoma empetrifolia*, and snowberries *Gaultheria depressa* and *G. macrostigma*. All are members of the heath family and all produce berries, red, white or pink. The two snowberries, once in separate genera, have been grouped in the same genus because they hybridise.

The commonest member of the lily family on Swampy Summit and Flagstaff is *Astelia nervosa*, whose stiffly arching, silver-tinged leaves form clumps up to 1m across. Its orange berries are inconspicuous compared to the bold fruiting of its relative, the bush lily *Astelia fragrans*. Among the mountain daisies, the commonest is a narrow-leaved species resembling *Celmisia gracilenta*, which has

OPPOSITE: Clumps of the giant speargrass *Aciphylla scott-thomsonii*, bearing flower heads over 2m tall, on the northern slopes of Swampy Summit, facing the Silver Stream catchment and the Silver Peaks. NP

Flowers and fruit: An undescribed narrow-leaved celmisia daisy (TOP), common on damper sites on Swampy Summit, and (BOTTOM) the showy fruit of *Pentachondra pumila* surrounded by *Gaultheria macrostigma* and *Androstoma empetrifolia*. NP

THE PAINTED FOREST

The 75ha Painted Forest is the largest patch of silver beech left in the Silver Peaks, a pure stand reaching an altitude of 700m, west of the tallest peak – Silver Peak No. 2 (777m). A dark green island in a tawny sea of tussock, it provides graphic evidence of the way vegetation can change with a shift in rock types. It is located on schist soils close to the boundary with volcanic landforms, where podocarp and broadleaved trees predominate. The Painted Forest and other silver beech remnants in the Silver Peaks are spreading very slowly, with seedlings softening the margin of the mature trees. The Silver Peaks marks a climatic boundary, too, with the land to the west becoming drier and less influenced by coastal conditions. NP

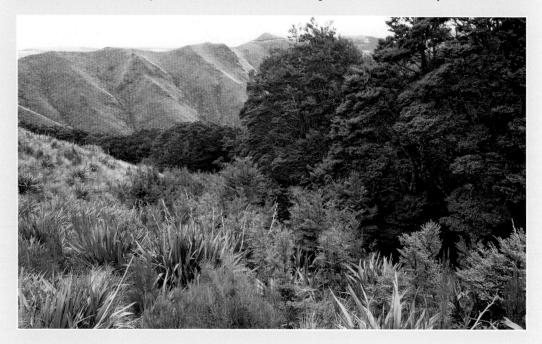

delicately petalled white flowers and may be found dotted about in open spaces. It is often seen in the company of the Māori onion *Bulbinella angustifolia*, whose yellow flowerheads are prominent in early summer, and the native harebell *Wahlenbergia albomarginata*, which can have white or pale blue flowers.

Damper places, including moist banks, allow the ubiqitous fern kiokio *Blechnum novae-zelandiae* to display its attractive reddish foliage. Also present is the rhizomatous *Gunnera monoica*.

Around the Swampy Summit bogs prominent plant species include the cushions of comb sedge *Oreobolus strictus* and the native anemone *A. tenuicaulis*, with *Kelleria laxa* occupying slightly drier sites. Strangely, the more widespread *K. dieffenbachii* is absent here but it is common on other low alpine areas and areas of exposed peat with wood remains of pink pine and occasional rounded quartz pebbles – actually moa gizzard stones. Moa swallowed small stones to assist them in the digestion of fibrous plant material, and over time these became rounded like river-worn stones.

ABOVE LEFT: View south from the Mt Watkin summit, across rock scree and towards part of Garden Bush reserve. NP

Two species of gingidia in flower. TOP: A greyer shade of green, *Gingidia grisea*, is an eastern Otago species. *Gingidia montana* (ABOVE), has only one population left in the Dunedin region, on Mopanui near Orokonui Ecosanctuary, but is still plentiful in the wetter mountains of the Main Divide.

Rory Logan / Peter Johnson

MT WATKIN | HIKAROROA

Mt Watkin or Hikaroroa, 8km west of Waikouaiti and 616m above sea level, is an oddity – a volcanic hill standing alone amidst a schist landscape, advertising its volcanic origins with an impressive series of radiating basalt boulder screes. Not only is the landform special; the slopes of Mt Watkin also contain some rare and peculiar plants.

Speargrasses abound, protected from grazing by Mt Watkin's status as a water reserve. The slender-leaved and palatable speargrass *Aciphylla subflabellata* occurs here along with the larger bluish-green *A. glaucescens* and golden *A. aurea*. Also present is *Fuchsia perscandens*, a scrambling relative of the high-profile tree fuchsia *F. excorticata*. The scrambling species has smaller, rounder, well-spaced leaves and smaller (10mm) flowers from which deep purple berries form.

Another uncommon plant, clinging to the rock bluffs of Mt Watkin, is a newly described native aniseed *Gingidia grisea*, now rare where grazing animals have access to it. This eastern Otago species is a compact plant with blue-green foliage.

New Zealand's only deciduous coprosma, *C. virescens*, occurs on Mt Watkin. It has distinctive orange-fawn bark on its branches and a trunk that often bears smooth knobbles. The leaves are pale green (as its species name suggests), thin and trowel-shaped. Dunedin is the type locality for this shrub, which is found from Gisborne southwards, especially east of the South Island's Main Divide.

On the more stable 'rock glaciers', patches of low forest have established, with broadleaf *Griselinia littoralis* and kōhūhū *Pittosporum tenuifolium* forming the bulk of the canopy. Beneath the canopy, moss and hound's tongue fern cover the boulders. Remnant logs of tōtara testify to the forest cover in prehuman times.

In 2004 the City Council bought the leasehold land around Mt Watkin and created a scenic reserve to protect the landmark's special flora and fauna.

ABOVE: Broadleaf *Griselinia littoralis* forest establishing on one of the rock glaciers on Mt Watkin. NP

LICHENS

There are some 1800 known kinds of lichens in New Zealand, several hundred of which are represented in the Dunedin region. Among the more distinctive species are:

Steinera sorediata: pale blue-grey, fan-shaped, found on rocks near the summit of Mt Cargill, from where it was described in 1963. A disjunct population occurs on Mt Taranaki.

Icmadophila splachnirima: pale green, rounded, found on subalpine exposure of peat on Swampy Summit, Silver Peaks and Maungātua. The species also occurs at Seaward Moss near Invercargill and Stewart Island.

Often the first plants to colonise bare ground, lichens are extraordinarily hardy and adaptable. They are found anywhere between sea level and the highest mountains. Their biology is complex. The fungal component depends on the algal one for energy from photosynthesis and in turn provides the algae with a cosy environment. Thus lichens are ecosystems in themselves rather than single organisms. Some lichens fix nitrogen in forest and grassland settings.

PIPIT – INSECT EATER

The insect-eating New Zealand pipit (pihoihoi) *Anthus novaeseelandiae* is commonly seen in tussock grassland areas, attracting attention by the way it flicks its tail. It runs with a dipping motion and flies swiftly. Because of its mottled brown colouring, the pipit is often confused with another bird of the uplands, the skylark, introduced from Britain in the nineteenth century. The pipit is more slender, with a longer, finer bill and no crest. It does not hover like the skylark, whose warbling flight song is distinctive, and it is less likely to be seen over pasture. Both birds nest on the ground, concealing their nests. A pipit's nest is especially hard to find. George Chance

ABOVE: A typical shrubland gully of Sutton Stream, where the dominant species are *Coprosma propinqua* and *Muehlenbeckia complexa*. NP

ABOVE: On cracked mud near the Sutton Salt Lake shoreline are mats of the salt-tolerant *Chenopodium ambiguum*. NP

SUTTON SALT LAKE | WORTH ITS SALT

New Zealand's only inland salt lake worthy of the name is located at the south end of the Strath Taieri Valley amid the spectacular tor ridges of Sutton.

Protected since 1991 within a 140ha scenic reserve, Sutton Salt Lake occupies an enclosed shallow basin in the schist landscape, 250m above sea level. Its water is about half as salty as seawater. The salts emanate from the schist rocks, arriving at the lake with surface run-off or by percolating up through the soil. The lake sediments are extremely alkaline.

Reaching a depth of only about 30cm, the lake evaporates in dry spells to become a cracked bed of silt. Salt-tolerant plants line the shore, notably the creeping herbs *Lilaeopsis novae-zelandiae* (type locality, Tomahawk), the chickweed relative *Chenopodium ambiguum*, native celery *Apium prostratum* and remuremu *Selliera microphylla*, the first three of which are common at the sea coast. Their presence 45km inland has had scientists speculating as to how they got here – whether they might represent an ancient marine shore (the sea could have been this far inland during the Miocene some 20 million years ago) or whether they were brought by sea birds such as black-backed gulls, which are not uncommon here.

No fish live in the lake, but there are tiny salt-adapted aquatic animals, including copepods, rotifers and water beetles – an attraction for ducks and wading birds, including New Zealand shoveler, mallard, paradise shelduck, pied stilt, South Island pied oystercatcher, black swan and white-faced heron. The Australasian

ABOVE: The speargrass *Aciphylla subflabellata* is making a comeback in the protected grasslands of Sutton Salt Lake Scenic Reserve. Rory Logan

ABOVE: Sutton Salt Lake. NP

ABOVE: An undescribed native forget-me-not (*Myosotis* species) is found on tor ledges among lichens at Sutton Salt Lake Scenic Reserve. Its only other locations are the Lammermoor Range and the Nenthorn–Macraes area. Rory Logan

harrier and spur-winged plover are also common. New Zealand falcons pass this way occasionally.

In the grasslands and shrublands surrounding the lake, native species are benefitting from the absence of stock. Among the five prominent native grasses occurring here (blue wheatgrass, silver tussock, narrow-leaved snow tussock, blue tussock and hard tussock), the wheatgrass *Connorochloa tenuis* is prominent. Palatable to stock and usually only found on the 'long acre', it is now flourishing in Sutton Salt Lake Scenic Reserve, decorating the grasslands with golden seedheads on long drooping stems. Also increasing is the speargrass *Aciphylla subflabellata*, rare in the region because of grazing. Shrubs of corokia, olearia, coprosma and matagouri form the core of the shrublands.

The moths and butterflies include the southern tiger moth *Metacrias strategica*, whose presence indicates relatively intact natural values. By late summer the dry grassland reverberates with the crackle of the small native black cricket *Pteronemobius bigelowi* and the larger short-winged katydid *Conocephalus bilineatus*.

Tor ridges in the vicinity, strikingly parallel when viewed from the air, have been exhumed by erosion. The rocks have weathered under the ground as well as at the surface, and the process continues. Only the most resistant elements of the rock remain.

INSECT HERITAGE

The Dunedin uplands have inherited a rich and colourful array of insects, some of which are possibly descended from species that inhabited the alpine zone of the cooled volcano, following the cessation of volcanic activity about 10 million years ago.

Underlining the long ancestry of the invertebrate communities is the presence of species with flightless females or with both sexes flightless, rendering them relatively immobile. Many species are active by day.

The key groups are grasshoppers, bugs, beetles, flies, wasps, caddisflies and moths.

Three butterfly species breed above the treeline in the upland and subalpine zones – an undescribed common copper *Lycaena new species* on muehlenbeckia and two tussock butterflies *Argyrophenga antipodum* and *A. janitae*. The latter is less common and faster through the air. The tussock butterflies may be seen flying together over snowgrass, the larval food plant.

Ground beetles (*Carabidae*) are another outstanding element of the fauna. Many tribes of this large family are represented in the uplands. Notable among the species is *Oregus inaequalis*, whose only known modern locality is Swampy Summit. Longhorn beetles use the widespread shrub *Hebe odora* as a larval home. Adults are common on the *Hebe* stems in summer. Another insect that uses this shrub as a food plant is the tiny and rarely seen diurnal moth *Scythris nigra*, whose equally tiny larvae do a lot of damage.

Two species of cicada of the genus *Kikihia* inhabit the uplands. *Kikihia angusta*, whose males are pale yellow-brown and females pale green, is common on the grasslands. A brighter green species, undescribed, is associated with shrublands.

TOP: The pretty diurnal moth *Cephalissa siria* is found where its host plant *Fuchsia perscandens* survives, notably on Mt Watkin and other hills surrounding Dunedin. A coastal population of this moth occurs at Akatore Creek, south of Taieri Mouth. BP

RIGHT: The carabid *Oregus inaequalis* on moss, Swampy Summit. BP

MIDDLE: The rare diurnal moth *Scoparia tuicana* was described from the 'Waitati Hills' in 1926. It has been rediscovered on Swampy Summit. Its only other known locations are Maungātua and Slopedown Range in the Catlins. It is at home in wetlands or damp snowgrass areas. BP

LOWER RIGHT: This recently discovered stonefly species *Nesoperla patricki* lives in copper tussock. Both adults and larvae use the moist habitat deep within the tussock. A wingless species, it is known only from Swampy Summit and the Old Man Range. By contrast, most other stonefly species are associated with flowing fresh water. BP

BOTTOM: The longhorn beetle *Mesolamia marmorata* was described from the Dunedin area, where it is locally common on *Hebe odora* shrubs. BP

TOP: One of the most ancient moths is *Sabatinca quadrijuga*, whose tiny day-flying adults appear on damp sites in September–October. They are common on Mt Cargill. The adults possess jaws instead of a sucking tube. Larvae feed on another ancient plant group – liverworts. BP

LEFT: Diurnal geometrid moths like *Dasyuris transaurea* are a feature of insect communities in the Dunedin uplands. Its striking patterning and bold colours are butterfly-like. The hundred or so similar species make up for a lack of butterflies in our fauna. The caterpillars of this species feed on *Anisotome aromatica*, with the adults emerging in November. BP

Two representatives of the order Orthoptera (includes crickets, grasshoppers and weta): a common short-horned grasshopper *Paprides dugdalei* (MIDDLE) and an undescribed cave weta that lives in tunnels in sphagnum moss (LEFT). BP

BOTTOM: The diurnal moth *Notoreas elegans*, formally described in 2010, is found in upland tussock grassland habitats on Flagstaff, Swampy Summit, Maungātua and Taieri Ridge as well as further inland on the Lammermoor and Rock and Pillar Ranges. The host plant for this moth and seven others in the same genus is pimelea. Typically, all of them vibrate their wings when settling on a flower to feed. Their wingspan is about 15mm. BP

LARGE SKINKS AT RISK

In the rocky uplands of the Macraes Flat, Nenthorn and southern Strath Taieri areas live populations of two of New Zealand's rarest, largest and most attractive skinks – the Otago skink *Oligosoma otagense* and the closely related grand skink *Oligosoma grande*.

Both have glossy metallic black skin with gold markings. Both bask on schist outcrops on sunny days, waiting to catch passing flies, moths and other invertebrates. They grab prey in their mouths. Crevices in the rocks provide hiding places and frost-free homes for the skinks. Their diet is thought to include a range of fruit from *Coprosma* bushes and the porcupine shrub *Melicytus alpinus*. Lizards may well play a seed-dispersing role for the porcupine shrub, which secretes its white berries among spiny branches, making them unavailable to birds.

The Otago skink is the larger of the two species, reaching 30cm in length, including tail, and 71g in weight. They give birth to two or three live young in early autumn. In warmer countries, lizards usually lay eggs. Live birth is probably a response to a cold climate.

The skinks are known to move between rock outcrops. One marked Otago skink moved 70m in two weeks, and a grand skink was observed to move 139m. Movement over pasture rather than through tussock grassland may make them more vulnerable to predators. Australasian harrier and New Zealand falcon are natural predators; the wild cat is probably the most dangerous introduced predator, although magpies, ferrets, stoats and rats are also likely to prey on them.

Last century Otago and grand skinks were found across Otago, having been reported from Rough Ridge, Roxburgh and Queenstown. Now their distribution is limited and scattered, and their future uncertain without proactive attempts to conserve them. Their two remaining strongholds are the Strath Taieri–Macraes uplands and the Lindis Pass–Hawea district. The Otago skink's plight is serious, with fewer than 2000 left.

RIGHT: An Otago skink sunbathing and waiting for prey on a schist crevice, beside some porcupine shrub *Melicytus alpinus*. NP

ABOVE: Tussock grassland on Hummock (736m) in the Nenthorn area near the city's northern boundary. BP

ABOVE: A lively grand skink among *Xanthoparmelia* lichen. NP

Features of the Taieri.
Bottom to top: Bulrush
or raupo, flax-lined
wetlands, grey ducks,
Taieri Gorge Railway,
New Zealand falcon
or karearea. Chris Gaskin

| # THE TAIERI

WHERE FALCONS FLY

RIVERS constitute the lifeblood of many cities. Unquestionably, the Taieri River is the Dunedin area's main artery. Together with its many tributaries, the river is at once a water supply (for homes and farms), a playground (angling, boating, swimming), a tourist attraction (Taieri Gorge Railway) and a landscape feature whose moods vary from raw and boisterous to utterly placid. Then there are its intrinsic values – attendant plant and animal life, some of it unique, with ancestry older than the river, older even than the hills and ranges that influence its course.

By the time it reaches Kokonga, the city's northwest boundary, for the run south through Strath Taieri, the river is already a seasoned traveller. Behind is the hot dry Maniototo Plain; ahead lie two plains and three substantial gorges. The gorges are Hyde, Taieri (Pukerangi to Outram Glen) and Lower Taieri, which cuts through the coastal chain of hills behind Henley, the final barrier before the sea. The Taieri's headwaters in the Lammermoor Range are little more than 40km from the sea. But the Rock and Pillar Range blocks direct access to the sea, forcing the river to meander north through the Maniototo until it can find a way around the end of the range at Kokonga. From here it takes a reciprocal course south down the eastern side of the range. By the time it reaches Taieri Mouth, 15km south of Brighton, the river has clocked up 318km. That makes it New Zealand's third longest river, equal with the Whanganui. Only the Waikato and Clutha Rivers are longer.

BELOW: Taieri River headwaters high up in the Lammermoor Range. NP

POETIC TRIBUTE

James K. Baxter captured something of the river's life when he wrote in his 1961 poem, 'At Taieri Mouth':

Flax-pods unload
*   their pollen*

Above the steel-bright
*   cauldron*

Of Taieri, the old water-
*   dragon*

Sliding out from a stone
*   gullet*

The Taieri drains 5650 square kilometres of Otago – about 18 per cent of the region. Almost a quarter of the catchment is over 900m above sea level. The lower end of the Taieri Plain, though, is close to sea level – a few areas are even below it – and here the river becomes sluggish. A flood protection scheme channels it, anticipating heavy rainfall in the hinterland and a consequent muddy torrent. There is a major flood every few years. Farming and the river have an uneasy relationship on the lower Taieri Plain, which was once an extensive swamp.

Dunedin's largest lakes – Mahinerangi, Loganburn Reservoir, Waipori and Waihola – form part of the catchment. The last two are basically natural; Mahinerangi is a product of a hydroelectric scheme on the Waipori River, and the Loganburn Reservoir feeds a power station and irrigation scheme on the Maniototo, where rainfall is under 500mm a year.

Taieri Mouth is the end of the line for the river, which discharges more or less directly to sea. Not for this river a wallow in an estuary.

The Taieri is tidal for about 15km. Spring tides push as far as Otokia and Lake Waihola. The river's Māori name – more properly, Taiari – refers to a particular tide. Early Māori knew well the link between the tide and phases of the moon and they had names for each phase and degree of tide. They named the river Taiari after the tide on the moon's eleventh night.

THE SECRET LIFE OF GALAXIIDS

Galaxiids are native freshwater fish widely distributed in New Zealand, including the Chatham Islands and the subantarctic islands. They occupy most freshwater habitats, including swamps, lakes, rivers and mountain streams. Their ancestry goes back tens of millions of years to the break-up of the southern supercontinent of Gondwana.

The best-known galaxiids form the whitebait catch in spring, chiefly inaka *Galaxias maculatus*, the adults of which inhabit swamps and low-lying backwaters.

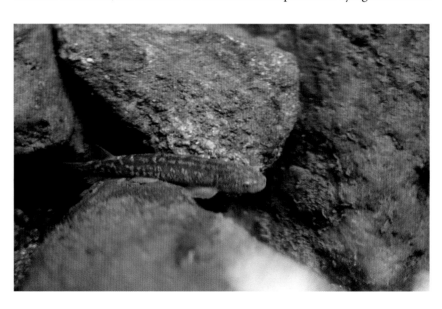

RIGHT: The lower Taieri galaxiid, *Galaxias eldoni*, which grows to about 15cm in length and 35g in weight. The structure of its fins is a chief distinguishing characteristic. NP

Four other species – kōaro *G. brevipinnis*, banded kōkopu *G. fasciatus*, and the rarer giant kōkopu *G. argenteus* and short-jawed kōkopu *G. postvectis* – make up the whitebait catch. The juveniles of these species, after spawning in estuarine areas and washing seaward, live at sea for a few months before returning to the rivers to grow into adults. All species except short-jawed are found in the Dunedin area.

Other galaxiid species do not migrate. They remain in their chosen niche the year round. A distinguishing feature of the galaxiids is their lack of scales. Few people ever see these native fish as adults because of their effective camouflage, their shyness (kōkopu especially) and their choice of bush-clad and forested backwaters as habitat. Except for giant kōkopu, which can grow to an impressive 58cm in length, they tend to be much smaller than introduced trout, with whom they are now forced to share their habitats.

The Taieri and its tributaries are home to both migratory and non-migratory species of galaxiid. There are four non-migratory species, reaching lengths of up to 15cm. All four are restricted to eastern areas of the Otago region, and two species have their main populations in Dunedin – Eldon's galaxias *G. eldoni* and Dusky galaxias *G. pullus*. Both are in the roundhead galaxiid group and have a 'nationally endangered' threat classification (the same as southern right whales). The stronghold for Eldon's galaxias is the Taieri below Middlemarch and the Waipori River tributaries below Lake Mahinerangi. The Waipori catchment also harbours populations of Dusky galaxias. They are much less shy than kōkopu, and adults may be seen swimming in daylight hours. Two other non-migratory species are found within Dunedin City boundaries – *G. anomolus* (roundhead group), which is found in the Taieri upstream of Sutton, and especially in the Kyeburn, and *G. depressiceps* (flathead group), which inhabits the Waikouaiti and Shag River catchments as well as Akatore Creek near Taieri Mouth.

These galaxiids have a lifespan of only a few years – probably just three or four years in the case of *G. anomalus*, and seven years for the lower Taieri species. Brown trout and other introduced fish have reduced galaxiid populations in the Taieri and elsewhere through predation and competition for food. In the Taieri at least, the native fish prosper only when trout are absent or in low numbers.

LIFE IN THE GORGE

River gorges such as the Taieri Gorge have acquired a refuge role for native plants, birds and invertebrate animals by offering steep, rocky and sometimes shaded habitats relatively unaffected by land development.

On either side of the Taieri Gorge the rolling uplands have been extensively modified by farming, but within the gorge significant areas of native shrubland and grassland, as well as pockets of tall forest, are still to be found.

The schist rock here is estimated to be 150 million years old. The hills are much younger and the river has cut down through them to form the gorge, the longest and most spectacular of the three gorges on the river.

In the lower sections there are stands of podocarp forest featuring kahikatea and Hall's tōtara. Kahikatea is very rare in east Otago. Inland, kānuka and mānuka form dense canopies along the banks. West of Hindon, conditions become

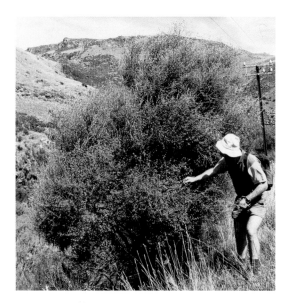

ABOVE: The newly described species of tree daisy in Taieri Gorge – *Olearia fimbriata*. NP

TEUCRIDIUM

Teucridium parvifolium is a small-leaved divaricating shrub growing to a height of about 2m. It is known from only three sites in Otago, one of which is the Taieri Gorge forest between Outram Glen and Taioma (Trotters Gorge and Gorge Creek near Alexandra are the other two sites). Its leaves are up to 12mm long, and its tiny flowers are pale mauve or white. It is a New Zealand endemic whose main populations are in Canterbury and Marlborough. Its square stems are characteristic.

RIGHT: Described in 2010, the cryptic moth *Izatha gekkonella* has its headquarters in the Sutton area where its larvae feed on lichens on the many large rock tors. The species is almost endemic to this part of Dunedin City but has also been found further north at Shag Point, Horse Range and the Kakanui Mountains. BP

RIGHT: Rocky stretches of the Taieri Gorge provide habitat for a large black noisy cicada *Amphipsalta strepitans*. As with most cicada species, the males make most of the noise, singing loudly to attract the attention of the female who responds with a wing clap. This gives away her position and the male then flies to her and mates. BP

distinctly drier and rockier. The vegetation reduces to scattered shrubland and tussock grassland. On the northern (true left) bank west of Hindon, there is an impressive shrubland community featuring kōhūhū, broadleaf (kāpuka), kōwhai and various coprosma species.

Among the indigenous shrubs and small trees in the gorge is a relatively rare *Olearia* or tree daisy. Small-leaved and deciduous, it grows to a height of about 5m and is found in greatest concentrations between the Deep Stream viaduct and The Notches. Prominent close to the railway line, it was discovered here in 1993 by co-author Brian Patrick and subsequently named *Olearia fimbriata*. This species was first recognised in the Upper Pomahaka area, about 100km west of Taieri Gorge, in 1986. A few scattered plants are known elsewhere in Otago and Southland, including a solitary tree on Otago Peninsula.

Below The Notches, between the railway and river, is a stand of narrow-leaved lacebark *Hoheria angustifolia*. Ferns, including bracken, are prominent

PARADISE SHELDUCK

Neither duck nor goose but something in between, the paradise shelduck or pūtakitaki *Tadorna variegata* is common in the Taieri Gorge. Flocks are seen along river or stream banks or in paddocks on the Strath Taieri and Maniototo Plains. They mate for life and are rarely seen alone. The female, which has a high-pitched alarm call, is easily identified by her white head and chestnut breast, belly and flanks; the male, which has a deep honking call, is essentially black overall. They nest in spring, usually on the ground under logs or tree roots, but also sometimes beside haystacks or buildings, and the 8 to 12 eggs are incubated by the female alone. Flightless during the summer moult, they were slaughtered throughout the country last century and in pre-European times, but their numbers have recovered. In coastal Otago there is a limited hunting season on the species, which affords a measure of protection. Elsewhere it is a game bird.

among the native ground-cover plants in the gorge. Flax is also found throughout the gorge.

Gorse and European broom are the commonest exotic woody plants, and the broom in particular is increasing rapidly to the point of threatening native shrubland. Wilding conifers – *Pinus radiata* and Douglas fir – are beginning to spread. A major threat to native vegetation comes from browsing by wild goats. In the past, clearance of vegetation by burning followed by grazing by farm stock reduced natural values.

There are two small plantations of English oak and Douglas fir next to the railway line between The Notches and Pukerangi. Willows line the river banks through much of the gorge.

In the lower, more vegetated parts of the gorge, there are native bush birds in abundance, including grey warbler, silvereye, South Island fantail and bellbird. In smaller numbers are rifleman, brown creeper, South Island tomtit, tūī, New Zealand pigeon and shining cuckoo. Black shags and southern black-backed gulls fly back and forth. The shags are breeding on rock ledges in the Hindon area, while the gulls have a colony a few hundred metres upstream of the Deep Stream bridge. The native paradise shelduck is increasing. Common introduced species are blackbird, starling, yellowhammer and the finches – chaffinch, goldfinch and greenfinch.

New Zealand's two daytime birds of prey – Australasian harrier (hawk) and New Zealand falcon – live in or close to the gorge. The more common harrier is frequently seen working the thermals round the clifftops.

ABOVE: A female New Zealand falcon at her nest site in the Silver Peaks area. One chick is visible, the other is mantled under the female's wing. George Chance

NEW ZEALAND FALCON | KĀREAREA

New Zealand's only endemic daytime bird of prey, the New Zealand falcon or kārearea *Falco novae-seelandiae*, may be seen anywhere along the Taieri River, although it is rarely observed downstream of the Taieri Plain. The Taieri Gorge is a stronghold. A pair nests every year on bluffs above The Notches.

Superbly quick in the air and agile on the ground, falcons hunt live prey, mainly birds but also lizards, mice and an occasional rabbit. Within territories that may range over 5 square kilometres they build nests – little more than a scrape – on rock ledges, and they guard them fiercely. Their rapid 'kek-kek-kek-kek' call is used in territorial and courtship displays and when swooping on prey or intruders.

Unlike the larger, slower-moving harriers, which avoid humans, falcons are practically fearless. They will attack people, dogs and tractors in defence of their nest. Females are larger than males. Over autumn and winter, the birds are solitary. Courtship and renewal of the pair bond occurs in July–August, with the male leading the female to the nest site. Two or three chicks are raised. They usually fledge before Christmas or in January and for a few weeks they are taught flying and hunting skills by the parents. A mid-air food pass is one method of instruction.

Being at the top of the food chain, falcons are susceptible to pesticides. They were often shot by farmers in the past for attacking hens and sheep dogs, but have been protected since 1986. Falcons based in the hills around the Mt Allen–Silver Stream area occasionally fly over metropolitan Dunedin, and sometimes they go 'window shopping' at the Botanic Gardens aviary, causing the caged birds more than a little anxiety.

LEGENDARY TĪ

The cabbage tree is found through much of the Taieri catchment and probably evolved in New Zealand on forest margins. Known to Māori as tī or tī kouka, cabbage trees were highly important in pre-European times as a food and fibre resource. Stems of young trees were cooked slowly in large ground ovens. Māori undertaking treks into Central Otago relied on it for sustenance. The remains of umu-tī (cabbage tree ovens) are found throughout the Strath Taieri.

ABOVE: The cabbage tree *Cordyline australis* in flower. One of our most recognisable trees because of its palm-like appearance, it often grows alone in the open. NP

AQUATIC INSECTS

Caddisflies and mayflies are prominent among the aquatic insects on the Taieri River, but it is in the smaller tributaries, and especially the headwater torrents and seepages, that insect life becomes diverse and highly specialised.

There are 36 species of caddisfly inhabiting the Taieri system, including the short-winged *Philorheithrus harunae*, described from the Rock and Pillar Range but since found elsewhere in Central Otago and Northern Southland. Lee Stream catchment hosts a local endemic, *Oeconesus angustus*.

Ponds and lake edges support an array of aquatic insects, including damselflies and dragonflies, backswimmers and waterboatmen, and several species of water beetle and midge. Compared to stream insects, these species can tolerate much higher water temperatures as well as less dissolved oxygen. Their habitat generally has luxuriant plant growth, however.

The larval cases of Leptocerid caddisfly resemble sticks and feed on vegetation and detritus in mainly stagnant waters. Adults possess distinctive long antennae and fly in a shimmering pattern over the larval habitat. They rest on pond or lakeside vegetation and are active at dusk or in the night.

Among the other orders, New Zealand's only dobsonfly *Archichauliodes diversus* – our largest adult aquatic insect – is numerous in stony montane and lowland parts of the Taieri where the familiar larvae, called toe-biters, are important insect predators. They hide under stones at the water's edge. The adults, which have wingspans up to 8cm, are conspicuous in flight at night.

Stonefly species are also common in the Taieri system and species diversity increases with altitude up each tributary and towards the river's headwaters. The larvae of all species are found in or close to the water, feeding on plants or detritus. Common in slower-moving and mud-bottomed tributaries as well as in the alpine headwaters is New Zealand's only scorpionfly *Nannochorista philpotti*.

Sedgelands containing flax and *Coprosma propinqua* are rich in bugs, flies and moths, especially if the pedestalled *Carex secta*, which has been called ballerina sedge, is present. Its skirt of dead leaves and associated litter supports the larvae of many species and provides shelter for adults.

The cosmopolitan moth *Scieropepla typicola* is responsible for the fluffing of raupō seedheads. Larval workings within the dense seedhead loosen the immature seeds, causing them to pop out involuntarily.

Damselflies such as the blue *Austrolestes colensonis* and red *Xanthocnemis zelandica* are found around stagnant pools. They are slower on the wing and less mobile than dragonflies like *Procordulia smithi* and *P. grayi*, both common here.

ABOVE: Among the larger mayflies in the Taieri catchment is *Coloburiscus humeralis*. It is commonly found in stony tributaries and montane to alpine sections of the Taieri River. Six other mayfly species inhabit the Taieri catchment. BP

ABOVE: Of New Zealand's four green stonefly species, *Stenoperla prasina* is common in the Taieri River and its tributaries. The similar but more purple-coloured *S. maclellani* is found in upland parts of the Taieri catchment. BP

WAIHOLA–WAIPORI | A WETLAND MOSAIC

By any measure – flora, fauna, water resource or landform – the Waihola and Waipori lake and wetland complex is a habitat of exceptional interest to Dunedin, Otago and the country as a whole.

The two lakes and their associated wetlands – a mosaic of streams, channels, backwaters, swamps, deltas and levees – cover about 2000ha at the southern end of the Taieri Plain. Although 10km inland and screened from the sea by a chain of hills, the system is influenced by the tide via the Taieri River, which pushes saline water into Lake Waihola. Salinity increases in dry spells. Both lakes are shallow (Waihola's mean depth is 1m, Waipori's 0.75m) and both are slowly infilling with silt.

Largely under protection now, the wetlands are a showcase of biological diversity. The largest populations of waterfowl in Otago live here, with no fewer than 11 species represented. In late summer, when moulting is in full swing, bird counts have reached a staggering 20,000. Altogether, 37 bird species breed on the lake shores and throughout the wetlands.

Black swans are the most conspicuous of the waterfowl. Populations of up to 6000 have been recorded here (see also page 75). Among the ducks, New

ABOVE: Channels, swamps and backwaters linking Lakes Waipori and Waihola (in the distance). NP

PŪKEKO

Related to the endangered flightless takahē and somewhat like it in colouring, pūkeko *Porphyrio melanotus* is a characteristic bird of the Waihola–Waipori wetlands. The size of a small hen, it can fly and dive but does neither very well. They are highly social birds, sometimes sharing nests. Fighting – done mostly with feet rather than the robust bill – is not uncommon to settle disputes about the pecking order. They move about the swamps and adjacent land in groups, feeding mainly on seeds, shoots and roots but also on small fish, birds or carrion. Flesh forms a large part of the diet of chicks, of which there are usually three to six. Food is often eaten from a raised foot, parrot-like. ROD MORRIS

FERNBIRD | MĀTĀTĀ

The Waihola–Waipori wetlands are a favourite haunt of the South Island fernbird *Bowdleria punctata*, whose habitat has been much reduced by the drainage of swamps since European settlement. Weakly flighted and nesting close to the ground, the fernbird is also vulnerable to attack from stoats, ferrets and wild cats. A member of the warbler family and about the size of the New Zealand pipit, it will fly for no more than about 100m at a stretch across dense sedgeland/shrubland vegetation. Its tail feathers are spine-like and often frayed, and the tail tends to droop in flight. It builds its nest in sedges and rushes, and the young, numbering two to four, are fed craneflies, moths, grubs and caterpillars. The Waihola–Waipori wetlands support a breeding population of some 250 pairs, making this site nationally important. The only other large Otago population is at Lake Tuakitoto near Kaitangata.

ABOVE: At the Waihola–Waipori wetlands, the spiders are preyed upon by resident fernbirds. The fernbird shakes the shrub to dislodge the female spider as she guards her nursery, whereupon the bird swoops in to catch the spider on the ground and carry it off to hungry chicks. Egg sacs are also fed to the fernbird's chicks. Paul Sorrell

LEFT: The nursery-web spider *Dolomedes minor* festoons gorse, broom and other low-growing shrubs with its distinctive white webs in late summer and autumn. The female guards her web and protects the spiderlings as they emerge from the egg sac enclosed within it. Males are almost as big as females and similar in appearance, with a colouring and patterning that makes them readily identifiable. These spiders generally live in paddocks and catch a variety of insects as food. R.R. Forster

Zealand shoveler or kuruwhengi is at home here. Over 3000 shovelers regularly use the area. Whereas swans are entirely vegetarian, shovelers feed mainly on invertebrates. They are the fastest-flying waterfowl and may move long distances between wetlands to feed and breed.

Among the less common species of waterfowl at Waihola–Waipori are the Australasian bittern, marsh crake and spotless crake. The crakes, weak-flighted and secretive birds, feed on small crustacea, molluscs, insects and their larvae, and the seeds and tender shoots of various aquatic plants. There have been very few sightings of spotless crake.

Once uncommon here, New Zealand scaup or pāpango is increasing in number at Waipori's Sinclair Wetlands. It is New Zealand's only diving duck. Foot-propelled, it can stay submerged for over half a minute and attain depths of up to 2m. It usually cannot recolonise shallow wetlands where dabbling ducks such as mallard, grey and their hybrids prevail; thus its increasing presence here is a tribute to the highly productive nature of this wetland ecosystem.

Waders are also numerous, especially white-faced heron, self-introduced from Australia, whose breeding in Otago was first confirmed in the 1940s. Pied stilt and South Island pied oystercatcher are reasonably common. Eye-catching cattle egrets, migrants from Australia, are seen in small flocks in late winter and spring. Occasionally there is a visit from a little egret, another Aussie migrant, or from a white heron on a lone excursion from the Okarito colony after the breeding season.

The herons are fishing, and the commonest small fish are the common bully, smelt and inaka *Galaxias maculatus*. Black flounder and lamprey inhabit the area, and yellow-eyed mullet swim in with the tide but do not reside. An ocean-going kahawai was recorded in Waihola in 1990 during a period of drought and increased salinity. There are good populations of introduced brown trout and perch. Green and whistling frogs are common.

For the birdlife, tall grasses, sedges, reeds and shrubs provide habitat for nesting, resting and escape. Dominating the sedgeland is the endemic pūrei *Carex secta*, whose droopy-leaved tussocks, mounted on impressive trunks, can reach heights of 3m. It is often associated with jointed rush, flax, toetoe and shrubs of *Coprosma propinqua*. On the margins of ponds, channels and backwaters are dense stands of raupō or bulrush *Typha orientalis*, which requires its roots to be permanently submerged. It reaches heights of 2.5m, and its upright sword-like leaves are strikingly green in summer.

Growing amongst the raupō and flax close to its southern limit is the swamp nettle *Urtica linearifolia*, a slender-leaved nettle extending its narrow stems to a height of 2m.

Among the trees that have established on levees and islands, kānuka reaches 6m in height and is commonly associated with broadleaf. Underneath, typically, is a shrub layer of *Coprosma crassifolia*, *Corokia cotoneaster* and European broom. saltmarsh ribbonwood and cabbage trees are relatively common. There are about 40 tree and shrub species in the wetland.

THREATS TO THE WETLAND

Dynamic and productive, the Waihola–Waipori wetlands may appear resilient, but they do face serious threats in the long run:

Siltation. The lakes and backwaters are infilling gradually with silt, which is carried in by the river, especially during floods. Die-off of raupō in places is symptomatic of this process. Since European settlement, the system has lost about 800ha to farm development.

Weeds. The crack willow *Salix fragilis*, introduced from Europe, will accelerate the reclamation if uncontrolled. Likewise, European broom will also threaten native shrublands.

Eutrophication. Run-off from surrounding farmland boosts nutrient supply to the point where algal blooms, which upset the natural food web by depleting oxygen in the water, are not uncommon. The Otago Regional Council monitors water quality, with particular reference to nutrients, pH, turbidity and dissolved oxygen.

Rock and Pillar identities. Top to bottom: Schist tor overlooking the Strath Taieri, cushionfield, South Island pied oystercatcher in *Celmisia viscosa* meadows, local endemic daisy *Celmisia haastii* var. *tomentosa*, female mountain weta *Hemideina maori*. Chris Gaskin

CHAPTER **9** | # RANGE ROVING

ROCK AND PILLAR, LAMMERMOOR, MAUNGĀTUA

ABOVE: Winter scene: Snow coats the Rock and Pillar Range to the valley floor in this midwinter view from Taieri Ridge. NP

Dunedin City's inland limits are alpine, spacious and singularly devoid of human contrivances except for an occasional hut or fenceline. They are the tops of the Rock and Pillar (reaching 1450m), Lammermoor (1159m) and Maungātua (895m) Ranges. Snow-laden in winter months and often well into spring, the summit crests and plateaux experience a climate that puts plant and animal life to the test.

The Rock and Pillar Range summit plateau – 23km long and up to 6km wide – has the most severe climate. The mean air temperature is just above freezing and winds buffet the place year round, averaging close to 30km per hour. The yellow-brown soils are moist, leached and acidic. Plants need to be tough, well rooted and low growing. Their growing season is just five months long. Conditions on the

RIGHT: Herbfield near the summit of the Rock and Pillar Range in early summer, with the 'Pillar' in the background. Snow patches persist above shrubland at the head of the Six Mile Creek catchment. NP

Rock and Pillar Range tops are only slightly less severe than on the high ranges to the west, in the heart of Central Otago.

Whereas the Rock and Pillar summit crest contains mainly cushion vegetation and stony or rocky ground, the tops of the Lammermoor and Maungātua Ranges are covered by a mixture of tall tussock grassland, shrubland and cushionfield. However forbidding the climate may seem compared to conditions near sea level, the alpine zone of Dunedin is species-rich when it comes to plants and invertebrate life.

New Zealand has an extraordinary array of alpine plant species, and for its area there is more diversity than in most other mountainous parts of the world, especially in the Southern Hemisphere. The species lists for Rock and Pillar, Lammermoor and Maungātua contribute to that alpine emphasis in the New Zealand flora. Among the Rock and Pillar plants are four that are found nowhere else.

On the Rock and Pillar, Lammermoor and Maungātua Ranges, the herbfield and cushionfield communities harbour over 150 species – a diversity that the most luxuriant lowland forest cannot match. Snowbanks add a special dimension – and challenge – to alpine flora. On the one hand, snowbanks bury vegetated areas for months on end; on the other, they act as drip-feed water supplies that last into summer months – mountain-top oases. The Rock and Pillar Range, being the highest, has the best-developed cushionfields and snowbanks of the three ranges.

Matching a diverse assemblage of plant species on the three ranges is a superb insect fauna. On the Lammermoor Range alone, there are 547 insect species in 13 orders – an outstanding count for a New Zealand alpine area. Some species are endemic to the range. Almost all are indigenous. Introduced species have barely penetrated the alpine zone. The Lammermoor Range and the uplands connecting it with the Rock and Pillar appear to be a sort of insect hotspot.

Typically for alpine regions, these insects are often larger, hairier and more brightly coloured than their lowland relatives. In addition, many are flightless (or sometimes the female is brachypterous) when kindred species are normally

RIGHT: Grasslands of the Rock and Pillar summit plateau, looking northeast across the Maniototo to Mt Ida (1692m), the highest point in the Taieri catchment. NP

ABOVE: From riverbed to range top, the South Island Pied oystercatcher nests in contrasting habitats. NP

MOUNTAIN-TOP TŌREA

Among the many paradoxes in nature is the presence of the South Island pied oystercatcher *Haematopus finschi*, a bird commonly associated with ocean beaches and estuaries, on the range tops over summer. Known to Māori as tōrea, it breeds inland – on farmland, riverbeds and alpine cushionfield or fellfield. The migration inland occurs from late July, although some non-breeders remain on the coast the year round.

Tōrea breed from about three years of age and usually pair for life. There are two or three eggs to a clutch and the chicks take five weeks to fledge. Over winter most birds move north, as far as Northland. Invertebrate animals are the bulk of their diet. With long bills, they probe for shellfish at the coast and worms and insect larvae in the mountains. Their calls ('hu-eep' or 'kleep', repeated) are distinctive and, on a still day in the alpine zone, somewhat startling to the visitor. Plump-breasted, they were a popular game bird last century. They are fully protected.

OTHER BIRDS

The range tops have a limited avifauna. Besides tōrea, two other coastal birds are regularly seen – southern black-backed gull (karoro) and banded dotterel (tūturiwhatu). Both breed in the mountains. New Zealand pipit (pīhoihoi) is relatively common and more often seen on the ground than in the air, running daintily or pausing to bob its tail. Australasian harrier (kāhu) overfly the summit crests on patrol for food, and most of the Rock and Pillar, Lammermoor and Maungātua alpine zone will be claimed as territory by pairs of New Zealand falcon (kārearea).

flighted. Diurnal activity is another feature of these alpine invertebrates. Perhaps their habitats are too cool at night; perhaps they are bolder in daylight hours because bird or reptile predators are few in number. Whatever the reasons, the fact remains that an array of strikingly colourful and surprisingly large insects greets the explorer of snow tussock and cushionfield. Despite their windswept and climatically rigorous nature, these mountain tops have a sizeable moth fauna.

The short growing season for plants affects insects. Their life cycles are often protracted. It may take several seasons of feeding for larvae to attain sufficient size for metamorphosis to adulthood to take place. This means some years are considerably better than others for viewing alpine insect fauna.

LAND OF TORS

The summit crest of the Rock and Pillar Range is a land of tors and strangely patterned earth.

The tors are sometimes clustered, sometimes standing alone, intact or in various stages of collapse. Survivors of millions of years of erosion, they are the most resistant bits of bedrock schist, rich in quartz. The loess and sediments that buried them, and the mica that helped form the bedrock, have long since been carried away.

The pillars are perhaps the most intriguing. Their upright, sheer-sided form is a product of vertical jointing. They inspire colourful names, these outcrops – The Castle, Stonehenge, The Window. Indeed, the whole range is named for them. Then there are the blocks that have split and toppled or lie tantalisingly balanced. Large plates of rock dislodged from the tors sometimes turn into 'ploughing' rocks that leave a furrow as they inch down a leeward slope, assisted by the frequent freeze-thaw activity and the extra water provided by accumulated snow during the extended spring melt.

On gentle or moderate slopes, the ground can take on a waved pattern of crest and furrow, rather like a recently ploughed paddock. These 'soil stripes' are caused

ABOVE: Patterned ground near Summit Rock on the Rock and Pillar Range. NP

ABOVE: Miniature ice-wedge tarn: Ice forming on this tarn on the Rock and Pillar Summit has pushed up a rounded bank on the downhill side. Alan Mark

ABVOE: Rock and Pillar tor – a Sphinx, perchance – and lenticular cloud. NP

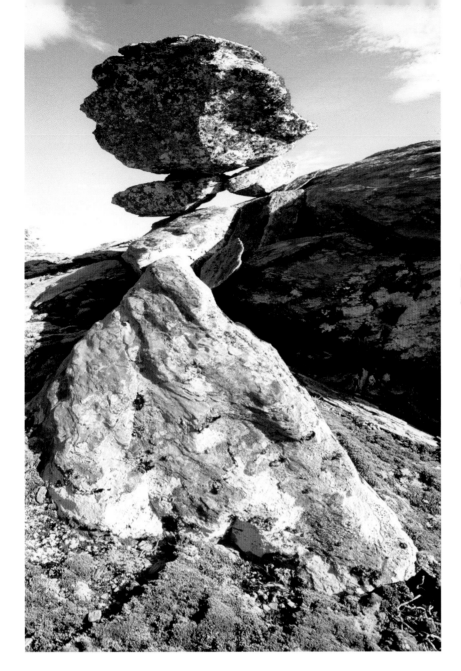

LEFT: A three-piece balancing act on the Rock and Pillar summit. NP

by the differential movement of soil and gravels induced by frost and subsequent thawing. When soil freezes it expands, and it moves again on thawing. 'Soil hummocks', another distinctive pattern, are usually found on flatter terrain.

Solifluction terraces occur when the soil turns to a stiff kind of porridge through frost activity and literally, if slowly, flows downslope across an often wide front at right angles to the slope.

And less than a kilometre north of Summit Rock is an intriguing landscape feature – a tarn that freezes over to create a miniature ice wedge. On its downhill side the ice has bulldozed a neatly rounded bank, a natural weir.

SHRUBLANDS

On the eastern slopes of the Rock and Pillar Range above the Strath Taieri is a well-developed shrubland belt. Squeezed between tussock grasslands and the herbfield / cushionfield of the alpine zone, the shrubland attains its greatest diversity and density in the upper reaches of the Six Mile Creek catchment. *Hebe odora*, *Dracophyllum longifolium* and *Ozothamnus vauvilliersii* are the most significant species, but no fewer than three podocarps occur in close proximity – snow tōtara *Podocarpus nivalis*, bog pine *Halocarpus bidwillii* and mountain toatoa *Phyllocladus alpinus*. The *Coprosma* group is represented by *C. ciliata* and *C. cheesemanii*.

At lower altitudes on the Rock and Pillar Range, but also to some extent the Lammermoor and Maungātua Ranges, the significant shrub species include inaka *Dracophyllum longifolium*, mountain flax *Phormium cookianum* and the tree daisies *Olearia ilicifolia*, *O. arborescens* and *O. nummulariifolia*. On the Rock and Pillar they grade into broadleaf / narrow-leaved lacebark forest in the gullies. Three groves of Hall's tōtara are known along the eastern face of the range. Subfossil tōtara logs have been found as high as 1000m and numerous small fragments of wood charcoal are buried in soil to the same elevation. Deforestation probably occurred as a result of fires lit by the early Polynesian inhabitants.

LEFT: Weta harem: A male mountain weta with three females. Their sheltering slab of rock was removed to photograph them and carefully replaced afterwards. NP

WETA | HONORARY RODENTS

By far the largest invertebrate on the Rock and Pillar Range is the weta *Hemideina maori*, which grows to a length of about 65mm. Part of the tree weta family, it has adapted to an alpine existence, spending the summer days under slabs of schist and nights out feeding on cushion plants and other insects. Males are easily identified by their bulging armoured head and massive claws; females by the ovipositor protruding from their rear end, through which they lay eggs. Males often guard a harem of females.

In winter and spring the habitat of the weta is invariably buried under snow. During these months they experience a kind of hibernation under the rocks. The existence of 'anti-freeze' properties in their blood (more properly, haemolymph) has intrigued scientists. Few animals on earth are known to tolerate sub-freezing temperatures for such long periods.

H. maori is found on other Otago mountain ranges and as far north as the Mount Cook region, but the Rock and Pillar populations grow to the greatest size. Their presence on predator-free islands in Lake Wanaka hints at a once more widespread low-altitude distribution. Their faeces, which collect under rocks, resemble rat droppings. Indeed, in the evolutionary scheme of things, weta occupy a niche filled in other lands by rodents such as mice and rats. The largest weta weigh as much as mice. A large ground weta *Hemiandrus focalis* is also common across the Rock and Pillar and Lammermoor summits. The orange-spotted cockroach *Celatoblatta quinquemaculata*, another prominent insect at high altitude, is often found in the company of weta.

BELOW: Three podocarps. Top to bottom: Mountain toatoa *Phyllocladus alpinus*, snow tōtara *Podocarpus nivalis* and (centre bottom) bog pine *Halocarpus bidwillii*. In the centre is *Coprosma ciliata* and at left bottom, *Gaultheria depressa*. NP

ALPINE INSECT LIFE

Matching the patterning of its snowgrass host, the grassmoth *Orocrambus geminus* LEFT, was described in 1991 from the Lammermoor Range where it was discovered in 1983. Some 25 species of *Orocrambus* – half the number of described species – have been recorded from the alpine zone here. BP

The female ghost moth *Aoraia orientalis* LEFT has reduced wings and cannot fly. It emerges in autumn and attracts the attention of the large male moths, which fly excitedly around it – a spectacular daytime event that often occurs at the approach of a southerly front. The larvae of most ghost moths live underground in tunnels and emerge at night to feed on grasses or mosses. Often called swift moths, they are an ancient moth group (Hepialidae) whose adults are non-feeding. BP

Geometrid moths have a triangular wing shape. They tend to be light-bodied, colourfully (often bizarrely) patterned, and active by day. Their larvae are mostly looper caterpillars and the adults behave like butterflies in the sunshine, resting periodically to sunbathe with their wings flattened one moment, then slowly waving or folded upright the next. There are about 30 diurnal geometrid moths on the Lammermoor and Rock and Pillar Ranges. Most are fast, elusive fliers but they require hot days to become active. The eight *Notoreas* species in the community vibrate their wings even when settling on a flower to feed, which presumably ensures they can take evasive action if threatened by a predatory tachnid fly. On tors at the northern end of the Lammermoor Range flies a new species of green-and-black *Dichromodes*.

THIRD FROM TOP: The diurnal geometrid moth *Dasyuris callicrena* inhabits low alpine shrubland on Maungātua, Rock and Pillar and Lammermoor Ranges. The elegant larvae feed on *Hebe odora* foliage and are well camouflaged on the stems. BP

THIRD FROM BOTTOM: Clever camouflage. The geometrid moth *Paranotoreas brephosata* is the most widespread of a group of orange-winged moths. They are masters of disguise. Predators are fooled into thinking they are chasing an orange moth, but when the moth settles it covers its orange hindwings and effectively disappears from view. BP

The exquisite geometrid moth *Asaphodes cinnabari* lives in damp herbfields at the northern end of the Lammermoor Range – one of its few known locations. It is pictured LEFT feeding on nectar of *Bulbinella angustifolia* flowers. Adults fly in early summer and the pale green larvae feed on herbs. BP

Worldwide it is rare for stoneflies to be short-winged and flightless, but this Otago-wide species *Zelandoperla pennulata* LEFT lacks wings completely. Instead it can run fast if disturbed from its habitat under rocks in swift upland streams where the larvae feed. BP

The black cicada *Maoricicada clamitans* RIGHT, pictured on *Hebe odora*, replaces the common grassland cicada *Kikihia angusta* in alpine areas, but is only locally common. The larvae are long-lived, feeding on the root sap for several years – possibly more than five years. In contrast, the adults live for only a matter of days, probably fewer than 10 days, during which time they focus on reproducing. Whether they succeed depends to a large extent on favourable weather. Males sing to attract a female. BP

The largest beetle in the alpine zone is the carabid ground beetle *Megadromus bullatus*, which reaches a length of 33mm and has a characteristic green sheen. A fearsome predator, it is found as high as 1100m. Beetles are the most diverse order of New Zealand insects and the Maungātua, Lammermoor and Rock and Pillar tops harbour a wide range. Many are diurnal, including the spectacular weevil *Zenagraphus metallescens*, which has a metallic appearance. Maungātua is listed as the type locality for 41 beetle species, thanks to a detailed survey of the range in the late nineteenth century. A flightless chafer in the genus *Sericospilus* RIGHT was discovered on the Lammermoor Range in December 1991, crawling over alpine herbfield at night. BP

The flightless chafer beetle *Prodontria montis* RIGHT, often seen in daylight crawling over the alpine cushionfields, is found only on the Rock and Pillar and Lammermoor Ranges. It is 12mm long. BP

This diurnal species of caddisfly, *Periwinkla childi* RIGHT, SECOND FROM BOTTOM, was first collected from 'under stones beside a torrent' on the Rock and Pillar Range (1280m above sea level) in 1981 by the late John Child. Also discovered by him on the Rock and Pillar are the caddisfly *Tiphobiosis childi*, *Zelolessica meizon* and *Costachorema hecton*, and a stonefly species *Zelandobius childi*. Aquatic insects are especially abundant in alpine seepages, snow caves over small torrents, and creeks that meander through the many wetlands. A total of 27 caddisfly, 22 stonefly and five mayfly species have been recorded from the alpine crests and slopes of eastern Otago. Some are flightless and have well-developed legs for running. BP

The stonefly *Zelandobius childi* BOTTOM RIGHT, lives in alpine streams on the Lammermoor and Rock and Pillar tops. Adults often have short wings and are flightless. BP

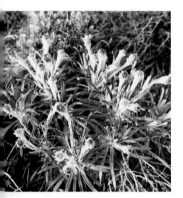

ABOVE: The Marsh marigold *Psychrophila obtusa* flowering on a snowbank, Rock and Pillar Range. Alan Mark

MIDDLE: The striking pink buds of *Celmisia viscosa*; BOTTOM: An expanse of *Celmisia viscosa*, spongy to walk upon, on the summit crest of the range. NP

ALPINE ZONE | A MINIATURE FOREST

Alpine conditions occur above about 1200m on the Rock and Pillar Range, where tundra-like plant life has developed on loess-covered schist. This is in contrast to the vegetation on the Maungātua and Lammermoor tops, which is established on extensive peaty deposits.

What some four-wheel-drive visitors to the Rock and Pillar summit crest might regard as a dwarfed, impoverished layer of vegetation is nothing less – to cockroaches, spiders and other ground invertebrates, that is – than a miniature forest and shrubland abounding in plants of diverse form, texture and colour. This is the world of alpine herbs, cushion plants and prostrate herbs.

A plant that specialises in occupying the highest and most exposed sites is *Dracophyllum muscoides*, the smallest of the 30 *Dracophyllum* species. Its species name refers to its moss-like form. It flattens its branches and foliage on often gravelly sites on the summit crests and, like moss plants, packs its leaves tightly to minimise damage from wind, frost and dehydration. It is a relative of inaka, the grass tree of subalpine shrublands and tussock grasslands, and grows much more slowly.

Other important plants of the alpine cushionfield include classic 'cushions' such as *Anisotome imbricata*, which is a member of the carrot family and produces carrot-scented flowers, *Phyllachne colensoi*, *P. rubra*, *Raoulia hectorii*, *R. grandiflora*, *Kelleria childii*, *Celmisia argentea*, *Hectorella caespitosa* and a newly described species *Abrotanella patearoa*, a moss-like daisy which is a local endemic. Another plant found only on the Rock and Pillar Range is a silvery green whipcord variety of the daphne family, *Kelleria villosa* var. *barbata*. The genus *Hebe* is well represented on the tops by whipcord species such as *H. hectorii* and *H. imbricata,* while *H. propinqua* is found sparingly in the shrub zone lower down on the mountain side.

The mountain daisy *Celmisia viscosa* is dominant on the Rock and Pillar tops, yet absent from adjacent Lammermoor and Maungātua. Covering large expanses with its tufted, leafy rosettes, it favours dips and more sheltered locations. Its species name (after 'viscous') refers to its sticky flower stalks. This daisy flowers irregularly, some years hardly at all, with a peak flowering in midsummer. It is joined by *C. ramulosa*, a needle-leaved species, and *C. brevifolia* on rocky sites, often in association with *Hebe buchananii*.

On the most sheltered sites, usually in snowbanks, is a daisy that is the Rock and Pillar's most notable local endemic – the variety of *Celmisia haastii* called *tomentosa*. It is superficially similar to *C. viscosa* but has lighter, greyish foliage, is more prostrate and is restricted to the late-melting snowbanks. Another daisy that is common and distinctive on Rock and Pillar snowbank margins is *Celmisia prorepens*, a Central Otago endemic, which has leaves that are broader, brighter green and less leathery than those of *C. haastii*. It is often associated in the snowbanks with the fern *Blechnum penna-marina* and the dwarf shrub pātōtara *Leucopogon fraseri*, whose orange berries are sweet-tasting.

Among the characteristic herbs of the Rock and Pillar alpine zone, and eye-catching because of their flowers, are *Gentianella bellidifolia* (white flowers) and

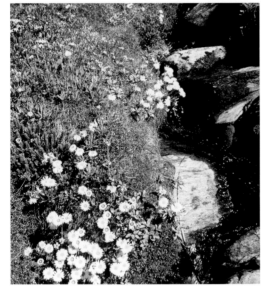

TOP: A needle-leaved daisy, *Celmisia ramulosa*, flowering among *Dracophyllum muscoides* and the white shoestring lichen *Thamnolia vermicularis* at 1350m on the Rock and Pillar Range in December. NP

ABOVE: The soft cushion *Kelleria childii* is abundant across the alpine and high alpine zone of the Rock and Pillar Range, where it hosts many bugs, weevils and an undescribed day-flying moth *Notoreas* new species. BP

LEFT: Rock and Pillar endemic: *Celmisia haastii* var. *tomentosa*, flowering in a typical location in a snowbank on the eastern face. NP

RIGHT: A cataract at 1320m near the head of Six Mile Stream, Rock and Pillar Range. NP

the buttercup *Ranunculus enysii*. The diminutive speargrass *Aciphylla hectorii* is also common amongst the blue tussock, with dense colonies on the McPhee's Rock end of the range. South of Summit Rock there are patches of gravel where the wind has stripped away the soil entirely, giving plants little chance of reclaiming this territory.

Lichens are significant in alpine areas. The white, shoestring-like *Thamnolia vermicularis* is abundant in places, as well as brown *Cetraria islandica* subsp. *antarctica* and blackish *Alectoria nigricans*. Small grasses are also abundant. They include blue tussock *Poa colensoi*, the worldwide alpine plant *Trisetum spicatum*, and very small plants of *Festuca multinodis* and *Agrostis muelleriana*. A small hooked sedge *Uncinia fuscovaginata* and members of the woodrush family, *Luzula rufa* and the cushion *L. pumila*, are common.

Isolated small patches and solitary plants of slim snow tussock *Chionochloa macra* across much of the summit crest suggest this taller tussock was probably much more widespread here in the past and could have been dominant when pastoral farming began in the mid-nineteenth century.

ABOVE: Tors on the summit crest of the Rock and Pillar Range. NP

SUMMER SOLSTICE MUSINGS
NEVILLE PEAT

It's 6.30am on the summit of the Rock and Pillar Range, Dunedin's inland edge, 1450m above worry level. The solstice sun has been bathing this high ground for an hour or two already, having caught the clouds napping. The schist tors extend shadows for up to 50m across the 'tundra', a pale green skin stretched thin across the cold earth. The ground-hugging plants must rejoice over days such as this, free of snow, frost and penetrating wind chill. True, there is a wind from the prevailing southwest quarter, but it is mild compared to the blizzard-makers that routinely stalk this place. Right now there is no snow at all on the summit crest, although ironically great banks of it lie at lower altitudes on the eastern faces of the range – fuel for mountain streams.

The tors are silent, decaying monuments to an unspeakably long geological history – weathered bedrock exhumed by the elements, the bones of the earth. You feel compelled to inspect them from every side, for there is bound to be an animal shape or something poetically abstract awaiting inspection. In the lee are microclimates – refuges for plants that are beyond their normal limits of altitude but are making the best of a chance translocation, their seed having been blown here or carried by a passing bird or animal. Lichens, less constrained than vascular plants and more practised at pushing frontiers, are more at ease. To lichens, a sheltered rock face is as good as soil.

It is a contemplative place at dawn, and quiet except for the whistle and whip of wind on sharply angled rock. Hardly anything moves on this bleakly beautiful, openly wistful landscape. It's too early for the moths and grasshoppers. They need a higher sun angle on their bodies and perhaps a higher air temperature to start up their solar batteries. On mountains you expect to hear water chuckling, but the summit crest is dry, almost desert-like, and suddenly your mouth is dry, too. The unfamiliar tugs at your senses – new smells, the unimpeded views, the vacant feel of the place. Without trees, distance is ready to play tricks. Is that rock outcrop half a kilometre away – or two or three?

Then a skylark calls from on high. The warbling voice is thrown on the wind – a salute to the sun perhaps, for why else sing so long and eloquently? The bird is invisible. No matter. It's the voice that counts, uplifting, convivial. The mountain is awakening.

HIGH LIGHTS | BRIAN PATRICK

Night has descended, clear and calm, on the Rock and Pillar Range. Among some shrubs near the hut, at 1200m altitude, I lay out my moth-trapping gear. Nothing too technical. There's a white sheet spread wide, upon which I place an ultraviolet tube connected to a battery. I wear a headlight – like a miner's lamp – and keep the butterfly net handy, ready for the first wave of nocturnal moths. I'm alone. My daughter and her friend are in their bunks. They had hoped to stay up and help but daylight saving in midsummer has delayed the darkness. It's now 11pm, too late for them. Oddly, daylight saving was first mooted in 1895 by George Hudson, of Wellington, who rather liked moth-hunting.

I stare at the blue light spreading across the sheet, and wait. It is a moment that will always excite me. Every light-trapping session is like a journey of discovery, and almost certainly no one's ever done this before at this spot and at this time of year. It's astounding how much insect life is abroad at night. New records and new species are always possible in a place like this. What will come in first? Invariably, the chafer beetles and porina moths are the first to get airborne.

Soon the moths are in a frenzy around the light. A species new to me flashes into the light. I lunge at it with the net but it's gone. Patience, I know, pays off, because the light is usually too much for them to resist. The new species returns and is bottled. For night-flying creatures that shy away from moonlight, they seem inordinately fascinated by this light. New research shows that their compound eyes are deceived by bright light and what they're trying to do is actually fly past into the dark spaces beyond. It seems their navigation goes haywire in the process and they end up circling and getting further confused. Most moths are simply recorded as they fly past or are released from the net after identification. The few that are caught I will pin.

Next morning I pin and set almost 50 adults, of which six species are new records for the range and two are new species to science, quite likely never before seen by humans. It's a special experience, light-trapping.

BELOW: A typical set-up for light-trapping moths. BP

LAMMERMOOR | TUSSOCK COUNTRY

In contrast to the Rock and Pillar tors and 'tundra', the Lammermoor tops, being lower, are essentially tussock country.

Narrow-leaved snow tussock *Chionochloa rigida* is dominant all along the 10km-long crest, which is broad and gently sloped and averages 1100m in altitude. In places the tussocks are densely packed and 2m tall. There are few expanses of *C. rigida* left in Otago that are as extensive and unmodified as the Lammermoor snow tussock grassland. Only around the highest points, such as Lammermoor Trig (1159m), do extensive areas of open cushionfield and shorter grasses prevail.

The Lammermoor crest and gullies blend into the Lammerlaw Range, which heads out at right angles to form the head of the Maniototo Valley.

Fires in the past are thought to have induced large areas of blue tussock, which, at the highest altitudes, is associated with cushionfield vegetation in which the main species are *Phyllachne colensoi*, *Raoulia hectorii*, *Anisotome imbricata* and *Celmisia laricifolia*. Two *Kelleria* cushion species are found on the Lammermoor Range – one common on the Main Divide and rare in Central and Eastern Otago

BELOW: Grasslands of narrow-leaved snow tussock *Chionochloa rigida* surround Loganburn Reservoir on the broad plateau between the Rock and Pillar and Lammermoor–Lammerlaw Ranges. The reservoir was created in 1986 on the site of the Great Moss Swamp following the construction of a dam and control gates for a joint hydroelectric and irrigation scheme. Countless invertebrate communities, including possibly undescribed species, were drowned in the process. A study of three sympatric (living in the same area) skink species in the Great Moss Swamp area in the 1980s led to the description of a new species *Oligosoma inconspicuum*, a southern New Zealand endemic, and a more widespread sub-species *O. nigriplantare polychroma*, in addition to the already named *O. maccanni*. Each species had a preferred habitat and distinct home range within the grassland community. NP

ABOVE: Flowing lines: Lammermoor tussock grassland. NP

(*K. croizatii*) and the other endemic to Central Otago (*Kelleria childii*). The former was quite recently found for the first time on the Rock and Pillar Range.

Between the tussocks there is another set of plants, including the whipcord hebes, *H. hectorii demissa* and *H. imbricata*, diminutive shrubs of *Hebe odora*, the straggling subshrub *Gaultheria macrostigma*, the large daisy *Celmisia semicordata*, and the easternmost plants of *Brachyglottis revoluta*. On the largest and last-melting Lammermoor snowbank (but not on Rock and Pillar) is *Hebejeebie trifida*, a high-alpine species centred on the Garvie Mountains and Old Man Range. Here, it is often associated with the native marsh marigold *Psychrophila obtusa* and the upland lily *Astelia linearis*.

Snowbanks are rich and extensive, containing a variety of cushion species, including *Phyllacne rubra*, patches of the daisy *Celmisia prorepens*, and the uncommon but highly aromatic glaucous herb in the aniseed family, *Gingidia baxterae*.

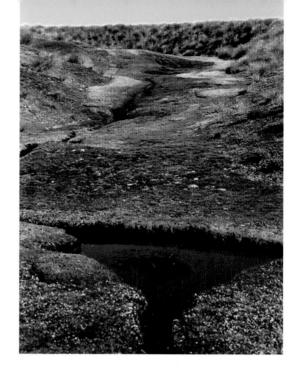

RIGHT: Colourful fingerbogs are common across the Lammermoor tops, and are home to many special insects and plants. BP

BELOW LEFT: A string bog near the Lammermoor summit ridge, the source of the Taieri River. NP

BELOW RIGHT: Stepped pools at an altitude of about 1100m on the Lammermoor Range. NP

RIGHT: On a bed of moss on a Lammermoor bog – *Utricularia novae-zelandiae* in flower. NP

Just below the crest of the Lammermoor, where it merges with the Lammerlaw Range, there is a stepped series of pools and fingerbogs that form the ultimate headwaters of the Taieri River. Cushion bogs include such species as comb sedge *Oreobolus pectinatus* and the sundew *Drosera arcturi*. There are broad carpets of the moss *Sphagnum cristatum*. The native dandelion *Taraxacum magellanicum* also occurs on wetter sites.

A considerable area of the Lammermoor tops, and arguably the least modified stands of snow tussock grassland, were acquired by the Department of Conservation in the early 1990s for a reserve following a tenure review of Halwyn Station. In March 2003, Te Papanui Conservation Park was opened, formally protecting 21,000ha of the Lammermoor area for the conservation of showcase expanses of tussock, herbs and associated fauna. The park opens up a range of recreational opportunities and protects much of Dunedin City's water supply.

MAUNGĀTUA | SHOWCASE FOR NATIVE PLANTS AND INSECTS

Although it is the lowest of the three mountain ranges within the Dunedin region, Maungātua (895m at the summit) has an impressive catalogue of natural values, and this is reflected in the number of times it has been cited as a type locality both for plants and for insects.

The tallest of New Zealand's speargrass species, *Aciphylla scott-thomsonii*, was first described from here. It is at home in the tussock grassland / shrubland environment near the top of the range. Similarly, both *Dracophyllum politum*,

LEFT: Shrubland near the Maungātua summit crest, featuring inaka *Dracophyllum longifolium*, the large mountain daisy *Celmisia semicordata* and narrow-leaved snow tussock *Chionochloa rigida*, which is flowering.
NP

which forms low hummocks on the summit, and the whipcord shrub *Hebe propinqua* were first described from Maungātua.

Narrow-leaved snow tussock *Chionochloa rigida* is dominant on the summit plateau. It surrounds bogs and tarns and mixes with shrubs of *Hebe odora*, which are prominent on all three ranges. The shrub zone extends down to 650m and includes the ubiquitous cottonwood *Ozothamnus vauvilliersii*, inaka *Dracophyllum longifolium* and mountain flax *Phormium cookianum*. Near the summit trig there are patches of inaka about 2m tall growing with *Coprosma fowerakeri* – a shrubland, probably climax, that predates European settlement and has been protected by bogs from fire.

Tarns and bogs on the summit plateau support sphagnum colonies. The bog pine *Halocarpus bidwillii* is notable among the shrub species, which include the mat-forming *Dracophyllum prostratum*, *Pentachondra pumila* and *Montitega dealbata*. Bogs and hummocky turf are colonised by such cushion plants as *Donatia novae-zelandiae*, *Oreobolus pectinatus*, *Celmisia argentea* and *Phyllachne colensoi*. Maungātua is the only Otago location for the lichen *Cladonia aueri*, which is found also on the Longwood Range in Southland, St Arnaud Range in Nelson and on Stewart Island.

BELOW LEFT: Maungātua cushion bog, dominated by cushion mounds of *Donatia novae-zelandiae*, mosses and lichens. NP

BELOW RIGHT: Wetland near the Maungātua summit, dominated by the moss *Sphagnum cristatum*, with the sedge *Carex coriacea* in the foreground. NP

As for the mountain daisies, *Celmisia semicordata* subsp. *aurigans* is relatively common and distinctive in the grassland and shrubland communities, occurring frequently in patches. *Celmisia densiflora* and *C. lyallii* are not nearly as common.

On patches of exposed peat west of the summit trig are old trunks and prostrate branches of bog pine and pink pine, silvery with age. Moa gizzard stones are scattered about.

The range has had a history of burning and grazing. Cattle have trampled sensitive bogs in the past. But the picture was much improved going into the twenty-first century. The Department of Conservation progressively acquired upper areas of the range and now controls the bulk of it. Actually, interest in conserving the natural vegetation of Maungātua predated the department by many years. Maungātua Scientific Reserve (553ha) was created in 1969 in response to a felt need to protect snow tussock, bog and cushion communities on at least one of the ranges of Otago. Such a reserve was first proposed in 1962. It is now linked with the Maungātua Scenic Reserve (273ha) at the northern end of the range above Woodside, which was mooted much earlier. It dates from the creation of a recreation reserve in 1889.

ABOVE: An exposure of peat, covered by decayed wood, mostly bog pine *Halocarpus bidwillii* – a scene typical also of the Lammermoor Range and Swampy Summit. Shrubland was more extensive in the past at these altitudes. NP

Conservation targets. Top to bottom: Otago skink on schist outcrop near speargrass *Aciphylla subflabellata*, New Zealand sea lion suckling pup, yellow-eyed penguin. Chris Gaskin

CHAPTER 10

CARETAKING
CONSERVATION IMPERATIVES

RIGHT: The iconic yellow-eyed penguin. This bird was making its way back to its nest on Green Island. NP

PENGUINS have stirred the conservation conscience of New Zealanders in recent decades. Yellow-eyed penguins have become a wildlife litmus test of our efforts to protect habitat and control predators – and much of the focus is on Otago Peninsula, a mainland stronghold of the hoiho.

These penguins have run an agonising gauntlet. Much of their habitat has been cleared away or burnt. Their chicks are vulnerable to attacks from stoats, ferrets, cats and dogs. In dry spells, fire can overwhelm them (as happened at the Forest and Bird reserve at Te Rere on the Catlins coast in February 1995, when a burn-off on an adjacent property jumped the fence and 52 penguins, half the local population, perished). On top of the dangers they face on land, penguins are vulnerable to problems in their marine environment. They can drown in set

RIGHT: Young face of conservation: Kiwi Conservation Club members erect a fence on Quarantine Island as part of a revegetation project on the island. Ken Mason

nets, suffer from periodic biotoxin episodes or become fatally entangled in plastic strapping.

In response to the hoiho's plight, the Yellow-eyed Penguin Trust, Forest and Bird and other organisations, not least the Department of Conservation, have made the penguin a conservation symbol nationally, and Dunedin is the focus for much of this effort – fundraising, education, revegetation, population monitoring, predator trapping, and acquiring new breeding sites. More than anything, the plight of the hoiho has emphasised the link between the wellbeing of a species and the condition of its habitat – basic ecology.

Nature is dynamic, thus conservation has to do with avoiding or buffering sudden change, while letting nature take its course. It has to do with keeping invasive animal pests and weeds under control, and ensuring that a representative range of natural ecosystems is set aside as reserves.

Not surprisingly, the larger biota captures much of the attention and caretaking, especially birds. Smaller, more cryptic fauna and low-profile plant species tend to get overlooked – and sometimes it is too late.

Species diversity in the Dunedin region – let alone the rest of the country – is so great that some insects and plants are disappearing before our eyes. Take moths as an example of local extinctions. Of the total of 834 species recorded in Dunedin, some 34 appear to have vanished. Thirteen are geometrid moths, the most notable of which is the orange-coloured *Xanthorhoe bulbulata*. This moth, once plentiful in eastern and central areas of the South Island, may now be extinct as it has not been seen for some 25 years. Its larval host plant is unknown.

Similarly, coastal *Pimelea* species are increasingly rare. The sand daphne *Pimelea arenaria* disappeared from Warrington Beach as late as 1985, together

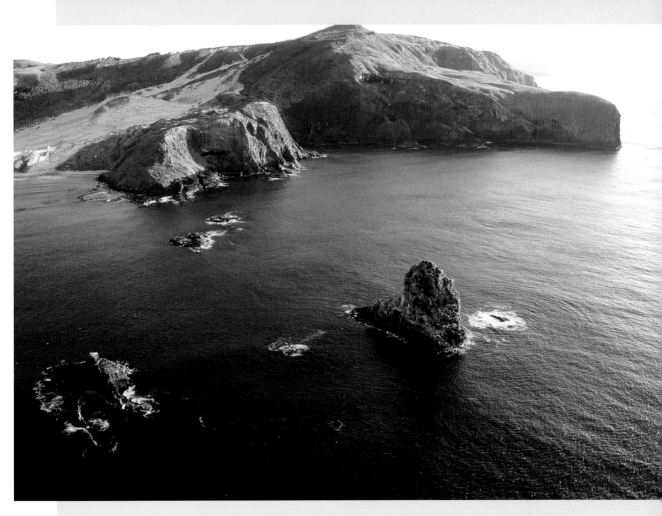

ABOVE: The rugged coast around Sandfly Bay, with Gull Rocks in the foreground, is a potential marine reserve. In the background is Sandymount. All the coastal land here is managed by the Department of Conservation. NP

NEW FRONTIER

The sea is a relatively new frontier for conservation. Whereas the protection of terrestrial values has long been accepted, the concept of protecting coastal waters is still not fully supported. Those with extractive interests generally believe the sea is sufficiently protected by weather conditions and fishing restrictions.

New Zealand's first marine protected area, where people may swim and dive but not disturb the habitat, was established at Leigh in Northland in 1975. By 2018 there were a total of 44 marine reserves in New Zealand, representing some nine per cent of the country's territorial waters. But protection is unevenly distributed across the country. Two remote island groups – the New Zealand subantarctic islands and subtropical Kermadec Islands – make up the bulk of the protected areas; reserves around the North and South Islands are spread out, generally small and not fully representative of marine habitats.

In 2014 the government set up a pilot project for marine protection focused on the South Island from Timaru to South Catlins. In February 2018, after three years of consultation and deliberation, the government-appointed South-east Marine Protection Forum made recommendations to government. Proposals for the Dunedin area included marine reserves adjacent to the city beaches and a number of protected areas allowing recreational fishing only.

with a moth *Ericodesma aerodana* whose larvae bind the leaves of the plant. Plants highly palatable to stock, *Gingidia montana* and *G. grisea*, both of which were once plentiful, are now found only where stock cannot reach them. Refuges include the rocky bluffs of Mopanui and Mt Watkin (see page 101).

Until recent times, native fish have been overlooked as a conservation concern. Like birds and invertebrates, they have suffered through loss of habitat and competition with (or predation by) introduced species. As can be seen in the Taieri River system, galaxiids have tended to lose out in competition with introduced brown trout. Research into the conservation status of galaxiids has pointed out the need to restrict the spread of trout. There is also a need to create reserves that target the conservation of galaxiids. Several upland streams, or portions of them, have potential as reserves – and there have been opportunities under the tenure reviews of pastoral leasehold land for such reserves to be created. For freshwater fish, habitat is not confined to in-stream values; habitat includes the vegetation on the banks, which shades the water and supports insect populations that help feed the fish. Trampling of riparian strips by cattle damages this vegetation and collapses the banks.

Clearly agriculture and forestry have transformed natural habitats, but the impacts of introduced plants and animals spread far beyond the fencelines and firebreaks. Possums, feral pigs and goats are

PARASITIC PLANT

LEFT: Parasitic plant thriving: An impressive showing of the mistletoe *Ileostylus micranthus* hosted by exotic trees on Highgate, Dunedin. Some native plant species have adapted well to city life, and this mistletoe is among them. It has disappeared from the North Island but retains a stronghold in eastern Otago, especially in and around Dunedin City. Birds disperse its seed. BP

A SAFE PLACE FOR PRIONS

The world's only mainland breeding colony of fairy prions (*Pachyptila turtur* or tītīwainui) is located on the sandstone cliffs just west of St Clair. Nature conservationist Graeme Loh discovered this unique population in the 1990s and began studying their breeding and survival. Rats have been the prions' main predator here. In 2010 the Dunedin branch of Forest and Bird decided to support a project to create a rat-free area for prion burrows by fencing clifftop land. This has increased the safe breeding habitat for the prions. A 138m-long predator-proof fence was manually erected by volunteers, with over 150 involved through the project. It was completed in 2013. An automatic speaker system plays prion calls to lure the birds that cannot find space on the cliffs to the new habitat. The species also breeds on islands and stacks around New Zealand, off Tasmania, southeast Australia and Chile.

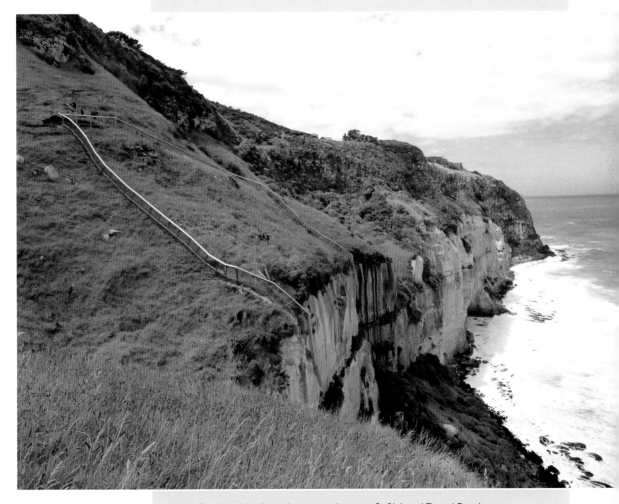

ABOVE: The fairy prion fenced sanctuary between St Clair and Tunnel Beach. NP capable of massive damage unless controlled, and gorse and European broom, however decorative their yellow flowers on hillsides, pose major threats to natural vegetation.

Possums on Otago Peninsula have been targeted for removal by the Otago Peninsula Biodiversity Trust since 2010 through a systematic and intensive poisoning and trapping programme spanning up to five years. With the help of landowners and communities, the trust aims to enhance the area's biodiversity by controlling or eliminating the main animal pests.

Wild pigs range through much of Dunedin's upland and alpine areas. They come as close to the metropolitan areas as the lower slopes of Flagstaff, where their distinctive and sometimes extensive rootings may be seen. They are partial to the tap-roots of speargrass, which belongs to the carrot family of plants. Recreational hunting helps keep them contained, but the damage they have done on the Rock and Pillar summit crest is of major concern because of the fragility of the herbfields and cushionfields.

Goats, many of them farm escapees or their descendants, have threatened native shrublands, grasslands and regenerating areas in the Taieri Gorge, Maungātua Range and the Mt Allen–Silver Peaks area. The Department of Conservation is systematically trying to keep the mobs under control. A technique used successfully in the Lower Taieri Gorge involves the placement of a radio transmitter on a goat captured live and released to return to its companions. Shooters, helicopter-borne or on foot, come back later to locate the 'Judas goat' and destroy the mob with which it is running. Deer are present in the forests of the Waipori catchment and sometimes graze on the Maungātua tops. Again, recreational hunting is helping to control numbers.

Not only has Maungātua had more than its fair share of introduced fauna, but it has also attracted considerable weed problems. Migrating slowly upwards, gorse and European broom threaten the protected areas on the upper slopes. A spray programme by the Department of Conservation has checked the uppermost infestations.

In some areas, notably Taieri Gorge, European broom is eclipsing gorse as the number one problem plant. Spanish heath *Erica lusitanica* is a threat to snow tussock grasslands in the Silver Peaks and adjacent areas, and nearer the coast, banana passionfruit and Darwin's barberry *Berberis darwinii* have been invading shrublands around Otago Harbour. In recent years STOP (Save The Otago Peninsula) volunteers have worked hard to control the spread of these and other pest plants and educate local communities.

Now that the term 'ecosystem' has achieved a measure of popularity and even won statutory recognition, conservationists can more easily argue for the protection not only of a particular native animal or plant but also of the ecosystem to which it belongs. This ecosystem approach to conservation quickened with the advent in the mid-1980s of the government's Protected Natural Areas Programme, managed by the Department of Conservation. Large blocks of upland and alpine areas have come under DOC control as a result of years of tenure review. A spectacular example is the creation of Te Papanui Conservation Park in 2003. It spans 21,000ha of the Lammerlaw and Lammermoor Ranges, protecting a nationally important region of tussock grasslands.

On Lammermoor's southern slopes is a 1000ha reserve whose name stands as an early landmark of tussock grassland conservation in Otago – Nardoo. Nardoo reserve was created in 1979 following a vigorous debate between a group of nine local and university scientists, led by Dr (now Sir) Alan Mark, and farm development interests. The scientists wanted to preserve a catchment with an altitudinal sequence of native snow tussock but an unsympathetic Land Settlement Board opposed the idea, and in the end decided the lower slopes should be developed as farmland. Fortunately, the upper slopes were protected. They include relic stands of silver beech forest.

Nardoo and Maungātua were among the first reserves on high country tussocklands. In those days the argument was over whether there should be any reserves at all; from the 1990s, as a result of a mounting conservation ethic and the rationale provided by the Protected Natural Areas Programme, tenure review and the nation's new commitment to biodiversity, the network of protected lands in Otago, and especially the high country, began increasing steadily.

Ecosystems inadequately represented in the Dunedin region include montane grasslands and shrublands (as on Taieri Ridge and the Nenthorn area), and snowbanks, low alpine shrublands and fellfield on the Rock and Pillar and Lammermoor Ranges. There is now also more protected land in coastal areas through Department of Conservation efforts and the initiatives of community groups, including the Yellow-eyed Penguin Trust. In 2008, as a result of community submissions and lobbying, the Dunedin City Council bought the 328ha Harbour Cone property, a working farm but also an area with significant ecological, landscape, recreational, cultural and heritage values. Native bush remnants on the Harbour Cone land have been enhanced since then through local people helping with planting and weed control. The council set up a community-led organisation, the Hereweka Harbour Cone Trust, to manage the property.

Community engagement on all matters to do with nature conservation is bound to grow following the transformation of the Department of Conservation in 2013. The department's new focus, in addition to looking after threatened species, ecosystem protection and work on national parks and other protected land, is to promote partnerships with local communities and the business sector in pursuit of conservation gains. In Dunedin City, the wildlife capital of New Zealand, there are plenty of opportunities to expand on the achievements of the Yellow-eyed Penguin Trust, Orokonui Ecosanctuary, the Otago Peninsula Biodiversity Trust, the Royal Forest and Bird Protection Society, STOP and conservation-minded organisations yet to be created.

ACKNOWLEDGEMENTS

The authors and publisher thank the Dr Majorie Barclay Trust, the Dunedin branch of the Royal Forest and Bird Protection Society and the Department of Conservation for their generous support.

For their assistance with scientific information we thank the following: Richard Allibone, Dr Barbara Barrett, the late Associate Professor Doug Campbell, Sally Carson, Professor Doug Coombs, Dr Brent Emerson, the late Malcolm Foord, Dr Ewan Fordyce, the late Drs Ray and Lyn Forster, Dr David Galloway, Tony Harris, Dr Peter Johnson, Carey Knox, Dr Chris Lalas, Shaun McConkey, Dr Peter McIntosh, the late Ian McLellan, Professor Sir Alan Mark, Dr Nick Mortimer, Lyndon Perriman, Christopher Robertson, Dr Richard Sadleir, Dr John Ward, and Dr John Youngson.

For the use of photographs the publisher thanks George Chance, Dave Curtis, the Department of Conservation, Brent Emerson, Ray Forster, Alyth Grant, Sean Heseltine, Stephen Jaquiery, Peter Johnson, Carey Knox, Rory Logan, Graeme Loh, Craig McKenzie, Alan Mark, Ken Mason, Rod Morris, Brian Patrick, Neville Peat, Lyndon Perriman, Paul Sorrell, Matt Thomson.

We also thank Chris Gaskin for his artwork at each chapter opening and on other pages. The drawings greatly enhance the book's visual appeal. Thanks also to Allan Kynaston for his maps.

The expertise of editor Vanessa Manhire and designer Fiona Moffat is gratefully acknowledged.

BIBLIOGRAPHY

Allen, R.B.: 1978. *Scenic Reserves of Otago Land District. Biological Survey of Reserves Report No. 4.* Department of Lands and Survey, Wellington.

Allen, R.B.: 1994. *Native Plants of Dunedin and its Environs.* Otago Heritage Books, Dunedin.

Allen, R.B. & Johnson, P.N.: 1982. *Vegetation of the Dunedin Town Belt. Botany Division,* DSIR, Dunedin.

Allibone, R.M. & Townsend, C.R.: 1995. *Galaxiids of the Taieri River: Identification, ecology and conservation status.* University of Otago Zoology Department report for the Department of Conservation.

Barratt, B.I.P. & Patrick, B.H.: 1987. Insects of Snow Tussock Grassland on the East Otago Plateau. *New Zealand Entomologist* Vol. 10: 69–98.

Bayly, M. & Kellow, A.: 2006. *An Illustrated Guide to New Zealand Hebes.* Te Papa Press, Wellington.

Beever, J., Allison, K.W. & Child, J.: 1992. *The Mosses of New Zealand.* University of Otago Press, Dunedin.

Bishop, G. & Hamel, A.: 1993. *From Sea to Silver Peaks.* McIndoe, Dunedin.

Brownsey, P.J. & Smith-Dodsworth, J.C.: 1989. *New Zealand Ferns & Allied Plants.* Bateman, Auckland.

Campbell, J.D.: 1985. Casuarinaceae, Fagacea and Other Plant Megafossils from Kaikorai Leaf Beds (Miocene), Kaikorai Valley, Dunedin, New Zealand. *New Zealand Journal of Botany* Vol. 23: 311–20.

Carter, J.: 1994. *Waipori Ecological District.* A Survey Report for the Protected Natural Areas Programme. Department of Conservation, Dunedin.

Cockayne, L.: 1911. *Report on the Dune-Areas of New Zealand.* Department of Lands, Wellington.

Dalrymple, H.K.: 1937. *Orchid Hunting in Otago,* New Zealand. Coull Somerville Wilkie Ltd, Dunedin.

Darby, J., Fordyce, R.E., Mark, A., Probert K. & Townsend, C. (Editors): 2003. *The Natural History of Southern New Zealand.* Otago University Press, Dunedin.

Dawson, J. & Lucas, R.: 2011. *New Zealand's Native Trees.* Craig Potton Publishing, Nelson.

De Roy, T., Jones, M. & Cornthwaite, J.: 2013. *Penguins – Their World, Their Ways,* David Bateman, Auckland.

Department of Conservation: 1993. *Lakes Waipori and Waihola Wetland – A Natural Resource Inventory.* Department of Conservation, Dunedin.

Dickinson, K.J.M., Mark, A.F. & Lee, W.G.: 1992. Long-term Monitoring of Non-forest Communities for Biological Conservation. *New Zealand Journal of Botany* Vol. 30: 163–79.

Dugdale, J.S.: 1993. Hepialidae (Insecta: Lepidoptera). *Fauna of New Zealand*. No. 30. Manaaki Whenua Press, Lincoln.

Eagle, A.: 2006. *Eagle's Complete Trees and Shrubs of New Zealand*. Two Vols. Te Papa Press, Wellington.

Fahey, D.B.: 1986. Weathering Pit Development in the Central Otago Mountains of Southern New Zealand. *Arctic and Alpine Research* Vol. 18, No. 3: 337–48.

Fordyce, R.E. & Jones, C.M.: 1990. Penguin History and New Fossil Material from New Zealand. In *Penguin Biology*. Academic Press, San Diego.

Forster, R. & Forster, L.: 2005. *Spiders of New Zealand and their Worldwide Kin*. Otago University Press in association with Otago Museum, Dunedin.

Forsyth, J. & Coates, G.: 1989. *The Dunedin Volcano*. New Zealand Geological Survey. Lower Hutt.

Galloway, D.J.: 1985. *Flora of New Zealand Lichens*. Government Printer, Wellington.

Gaskin, C.: 1989. *A Walk To The Beach*. Heinemann Reed, Auckland.

Gaskin, C.: 1985. *Remote the Land's Heart*. John McIndoe, Dunedin.

Gaskin, C. & Peat, N.: 1991. *The World of Albatrosses*. Hodder & Stoughton, Auckland.

Gaskin, C. & Peat, N.: 1991. *The World of Penguins*. Hodder & Stoughton, Auckland.

Hamilton S.A.: 1991. The Role of Sex Ratio, Spatial Distribution and Head Size in the Mating System of the Rock and Pillar Weta *Hemideina maori*. *University of Otago, Wildlife Management Report* No, 17. University of Otago, Dunedin.

Hardy, P.F.: 1982. *Pastoral Lands Assessment Report, Rock and Pillar Range, Otago*. Department of Lands and Survey, Dunedin.

Heads, M.J.: 1990. A Revision of the Genera Kelleria and Drapetes (Thymelaeaceae). *Australian Systematic Botany* Vol. 3: 595–652.

Heather, B.D. & Robertson H.A.: 1996 (revised 2005). *The Field Guide to the Birds of New Zealand*, Penguin Books, Auckland.

Holdsworth, D.K. & Mark, A.F.: 1990. Water and Nutrient Input:Output Budgets; Effects of Plant Cover at Seven Sites in Upland Snow Tussock Grasslands of Eastern and Central Otago, New Zealand. *Journal of Royal Society of New Zealand* Vol. 20(1): 1–24.

Jaquiery, S. (photographs), Michelsen-Heath, S. & Söhle, I. (text): 2005. *City Birds: A Dunedin Field Guide*, Otago Daily Times & Otago Museum, Dunedin.

Johnson, P.N.: 1982. *The Sand Dune and Beach Vegetation Inventory of New Zealand*, Vol. 2, *South Island and Stewart Island*. DSIR Land Resources, Christchurch.

Johnson, P. & Brooke, P.: 1989. *Wetland Plants in New Zealand*. DSIR Field Guide, DSIR, Wellington.

Johnson, P.N.: 1992. *Otago Peninsula Vascular Plant Flora*. Landcare Research Ltd., Dunedin.

McKellar, I.C.: 1990. *Geology of the Southwest Dunedin Urban Area*. New Zealand Geological Survey, Lower Hutt.

Mark, A.F.: 1994. Patterned Ground Activity in a Southern New Zealand High Alpine Cushionfield. *Arctic and Alpine Research* Vol. 26(3): 270–280.

Mark, A.F. & Adams, N.M.: 1995 (revised and updated edition). *New Zealand Alpine Plants*. Godwit, Auckland.

Mark, A.F. & Bliss, L.C.: 1970. The High-Alpine Vegetation of Central Otago, New Zealand. *New Zealand Journal of Botany* 8: 381–451.

Mark, A.F.: 2012. *Above the Treeline*, Craig Potton Publishing, Nelson.

Mason, B.: 1989. *Outdoor Recreation in Otago: A Recreation Plan, Vol. II*. Silverpeaks and Otago's Alps. Federated Mountain Clubs of New Zealand, Wellington.

Morris, R. & Forsyth, J.: 1986. *Almost An Island: Guide to Otago Peninsula*. John McIndoe, Dunedin.

Mortimer, N.: 1993. *Geology of the Otago Schist and Adjacent Rocks*. 1:500,000. Map No. 7. Institute of Geological and Nuclear Sciences Ltd, Lower Hutt.

New Zealand Geological Survey: 1969. *The W.N. Benson Map of Dunedin*. New Zealand Geological Survey, Wellington.

Oliver, W.R.B.: 1937. The Tertiary Flora of the Kaikorai Valley, Otago, New Zealand. *Transactions and Proceedings of the Royal Society of New Zealand* Vol. 66(3): 284–311.

Patrick, B.H.: 1984. Lammermoor–Lammerlaw: A Tussockland National Reserve in Eastern Otago? *Forest & Bird* Vol. 15(4): 7.

Patrick, B.H.: 1990. Occurrence of an Upland Grassland Moth in a Coastal Saltmarsh in Otago. *Journal of Royal Society of New Zealand* Vol. 20(3): 305–07.

Patrick, B.H.: Description of a New Species of Crambidae: Crambinae (Lepidoptera) from New Zealand. *New Zealand Journal of Zoology* Vol. 18: 357–62.

Patrick, B.H.: 1994a. The Importance of Invertebrate Biodiversity. An Otago Conservancy Review. *Conservation Advisory Science Notes* No. 53. Department of Conservation, Wellington.

Patrick, B.H., Barrett, B.I.P., Ward, J.B. & McLellan, I.: 1993. Insects of Waipori Ecological District. Department of Conservation, Dunedin. *Miscellaneous Series* No. 11.

Patrick, B.H. & Patrick, H.J.H.: 2012. *Butterflies of the South Pacific*. Otago University Press, Dunedin.

Patterson, G.B. & Dougherty, C.H.: 1990. Four new species and one new subspecies of skinks, genus Leiolopisma (Reptilia: Lacertilia: Scincidae) from New Zealand. *Journal of the Royal Society of New Zealand* Vol. 20(1): 65–84.

Paviour-Smith, K.: 1956. The Biotic Community of a Salt Meadow in New Zealand. *Transactions of the Royal Society of New Zealand* Vol. 83(3): 525–54.

Peat, N.: 1992. *The Falcon and the Lark*, John McIndoe, Dunedin.

Peat, N.: 2011. *Seabird Genius: The Story of L.E. Richdale, the Royal Albatross and the Yellow-eyed Penguin*, Otago University Press, Dunedin.

Probert, K. & Westerskov, K.: 1981. *The Seas Around New Zealand*. Reed, Wellington.

Richdale, L.E.: 1957. *A Population Study of Penguins*. Oxford University Press, Oxford.

Simpson, G. & Scott-Thomson, J.: 1938. The Dunedin Sub-district of the South Otago Botanical District. *Transactions of the Royal Society of New Zealand* Vol. 6: 430–42.

Shaw, T.: 1994. Population Size, Distribution, Home Range and Translocation of the Jewelled Gecko, Naultinus gemmeus, at the Every Scientific Reserve, Otago Peninsula. *University of Otago Wildlife Management Report* No. 56.

St George, I.: 1992. *Wild Orchids in the Far South of New Zealand.* New Zealand Native Orchid Group, Wellington.

Talbot, J.M., Mark, A.F., & Wilson, J.B.: 1992. Vegetation-environment Relations in Snowbanks on the Rock and Pillar Range, Central Otago, New Zealand. *New Zealand Journal of Botany* Vol. 30: 271–301.

Thomas, B.M., Minot, E.O., Holland, J.D.: 2013. Fledging behaviour of Juvenile Northern Royal Albatrosses (Diomedea sanfordi): a GPS Tracking Study. *Notornis*, Vol. 57 Part 3: 135–47.

Ward, G. & Munro, C.M.: 1989. *Otago II Biological Survey of Reserves Series* No. 20. Department of Conservation, Wellington.

Wardle, P. & Mark, A.F.: 1956. Vegetation and Climate in the Dunedin District. *Transactions of the Royal Society of New Zealand* Vol. 84(1): 33–44.

Whitaker, A.H.: 1988. A Survey of the Lizards of the Rock and Pillar Range Area. *Otago Giant Skink Survey* No. 8. Department of Conservation, Dunedin.

Wilson, C.M. & Given, D.R.: 1989. *Threatened Plants of New Zealand*. DSIR Field Guide.

INDEX

Page numbers in **bold** refer to illustrations.